Power
of the
Wheel

Power of the Wheel

The Falun Gong Revolution

Ian Adams
Riley Adams
Rocco Galati

Published in 2000 by Stoddart Publishing Co. Limited
895 Don Mills Road 400-2 Park Centre, Toronto, Canada M3C 1W3
180 Varick Street, 9th Floor, New York, New York 10014

Distributed in Canada by:
General Distribution Services Ltd.
325 Humber College Blvd., Toronto, Ontario M9W 7C3
Tel. (416) 213-1919   Fax (416) 213-1917
Email cservice@genpub.com

Distributed in the United States by:
General Distribution Services Inc.
PMB 128, 4500 Witmer Industrial Estates, Niagara Falls, New York 14305-1386
Toll-free Tel.1-800-805-1083   Toll-free Fax 1-800-481-6207
Email gdsinc@genpub.com

04 03 02 01 00 1 2 3 4 5

Canadian Cataloguing in Publication Data

Adams, Ian
Power of the wheel : the falun gong revolution

Includes bibliographical references and index.

ISBN 0-7737-3270-5

1. Ch'i kung.   2. Exercise — Religious aspects — Buddhism.
3. Religion and politics — China.   4. Li, Hongzhi, 1951– .   I. Adams, Riley.
II. Galati, Rocco, 1959– .   III. Title.

BQ5670.A32   2000   294.3'4   C00-931348-6

All photographs courtesy of the Falun Da Fa Association of Canada,
unless otherwise indicated.

Jacket design: Angel Guerra
Text design and typesetting: Kinetics Design & Illustration

The Canada Council | Le Conseil des Arts
FOR THE ARTS | DU CANADA
SINCE 1957 | DEPUIS 1957

We acknowledge for their financial support of our publishing program the Canada Council, the Ontario Arts Council, and the Government of Canada through the Book Publishing Industry Development Program (BPIDP).

Printed and bound in Canada

With thanks to the many people who helped us write this book.

Contents

"The religion of the future will be a cosmic religion. It should transcend personal God and avoid dogma and theology. Covering both the natural and the spiritual, it should be based on a religious sense arising from the experience of all things natural and spiritual as a meaningful unity."

~ Albert Einstein

Authors' Note

*I*n early 1999, when we began to study the Falun Gong phenomenon, it became immediately apparent that our task would be far-ranging and complex. Having researched the origins of Li Hongzhi's spiritual belief system and observed its remarkable impact both in China and around the world, we succeeded in interviewing many of his closest and most senior disciples, including his brother, Li Donghui. We also spoke at length with numerous ordinary adherents, who prefer to describe themselves as "practitioners." But despite repeated efforts we could not reach Li himself. As we will explain, he is thought to reside somewhere in the United States, and communicates solely by means of the Internet.

He was last seen by an impartial and reliable observer on July 22, 1999, and we have wondered at times if he is still alive. So jealously is his precise location guarded that two prominent disciples, Zhang Erping and Ye Hao, told us they didn't know how to reach him. Even his brother contented himself with carefully worded statements such as "I have no news of where he is at this time."

Various more or less plausible reasons for this veil of secrecy were offered or hinted at. Some people suggested that Li was in fear for his life, as the Chinese authorities had supposedly ordered his assassination. Others maintained that he was merely observing a "necessary period of self-imposed silence."

As our work neared completion, when we once again attempted to establish some form of direct contact we received (via his disciples) what purported to be a personal message from Li. It advised that writing a book about the Great Law — in other words, his teachings — was a "serious endeavour." If the results could "verify" the Great Law, he would do everything to assist us. If not, helping us would be a "crime." Our "good intention" was not the issue. An interview would only be granted, he said, if he could read the manuscript ahead of time. Then, if he approved of it, we could ask him questions. These terms were unacceptable, and our book is therefore in no way authorized by Li or his followers.

To explain Li and his movement to Western readers, we have divided our story into four chapters, along with this note and a brief prologue.

Chapter One describes Li's creation of Falun Gong, which translates as "Power of the Wheel." Falun Gong is also known, almost interchangeably, as Falun "Dafa" or "Da Fa," meaning — as indicated by the response to our interview request — "Great Law." This chapter includes a bare-bones explanation of Falun Gong's practices and beliefs and outlines its initial success within China, and to some extent overseas, a success that continued almost unabated until 1999, by which time Li had left China.

Chapter Two examines the brutal suppression of Falun Gong

practitioners that was subsequently imposed by the Chinese Communist regime. It illustrates how President Jiang Zemin's campaign was dictated both by present-day political considerations and by historical precedents and links the persecutions to other issues — in particular, China's attempt to join the World Trade Organization.

Chapter Three explores in greater detail several important components of Li Hongzhi's teachings and their roots in China's traditional religious systems, which Li has borrowed from to suit his purposes. It also contrasts his undeniable achievements with a selection of his more outrageous actions and utterances.

Finally, Chapter Four reviews the reasons for China's battle against Falun Gong and speculates on what tomorrow may hold for the nation, for Li, and for his unfortunate practitioners.

A friendly caution to Western readers with only a general knowledge of and interest in Chinese religious practices: Portions of our story will of necessity be somewhat heavy going. So will many if not most of the excerpts from Li's writings, which usually resemble a badly subtitled film. Bear with us, and we will strive to provide lucid translations as we go along.

We are well aware that our results will not please or satisfy everyone. Indeed, we ourselves are not in absolute agreement on Li's true colours, the relative importance of his various sources, or the subtleties of his message. At times, we found it difficult to strike a working consensus that would enable us to set aside our differences (which are for the most part matters of emphasis and degree, not kind) and concentrate on the facts as we've been able to ascertain them, to depict Li, warts and all, and let readers arrive at their own conclusions.

Li's true believers, of course, made up their minds long ago and are unlikely to be swayed by anything we have to say. We honour their beliefs, and hope that we have not offered them undue offence. Above all, we salute the boundless courage of

Falun Gong practitioners in China during their time of trial, and hope that we have not in any way belittled their sacrifices.

The problem in coming to grips with Falun Gong is that, even at the best of times, many Westerners harbour a limited patience for shades of meaning and ambiguous thought, preferring instead the comfort of easy absolutes: black and white, right and wrong, good and bad. But there are precious few absolutes when it comes to Li's fascinating, though sometimes maddening, movement. Readers with a taste for ambiguity will find a full plate of it here, starting with Li himself, who (to borrow Sir Winston Churchill's description of Russia) remains a riddle wrapped in a mystery inside an enigma.

One thing is certain, however, and here, we as authors are in complete agreement: Not since the days of Mohandas Gandhi has one man had such an enormous spiritual and political impact on his native country — an impact so forceful that the resonance of his message could not be contained within his country's borders, but spilled over onto a broader stage.

That having been said, the real debate begins. Li's ardent disciples would argue that he's a modern-day prophet whose global importance may prove equal to that of Jesus, the Buddha, Mohammed, or the Taoist Lao-tzu. They would also maintain that his teachings represent an ultimate truth. Li, who refers to himself as "the principal being," would concur wholly with this view.

Others go to the opposite extreme, suggesting that Falun Gong is in essence a cult, that its practitioners are cultists, and that Li qualifies as a cult leader or, failing that, a man whose grip on reality is tenuous at best.

A middle ground may be that Li, for all his contradictions, is an intriguing part of a Chinese spiritual continuum, one of a long line of men who for centuries have sought to synthesize for the Chinese people the "Three Teachings" — the great strands of Buddhism, Taoism, and Confucianism. In his book *The Joy of Sects*, religious historian Peter Occhiogrosso identifies a category of spiritual reformers who rose up at different times and in different places to demand a paring away of moral fat and corruption, putting their own ingenious spins on whomever and whatever preceded them. In this group Occhiogrosso includes personalities as diverse as the Old Testament prophets, the neo-Confucianist theoretician Chu Hsi, St. Francis of Assisi, the Sufi Muslim Mansur al-Hallaj, and the Ba'al Shem Tov (the founder of Hasidism). All of them, in Occhiogrosso's words, are linked in that they "worked to clarify and redirect the aims and practices of their traditions without rending the fabric." When the dust settles, Li may enter history as this sort of figure.

This seems plausible enough, but however we may choose to categorize Li Hongzhi, it would be perilous to underestimate him. History has shown that, in some cases, the radical reshaping of a religion does indeed rend its fabric beyond repair or recognition, culminating in the emergence of an entirely new and long-lasting belief that could not possibly have been intended or foreseen by its earliest followers. To cite one example, the Baha'i faith was originally an Orthodox Islamic sect, and suffered persecutions every bit as cruel as those that have been visited on Falun Gong's Chinese practitioners. It then broke off, became something altogether distinct, and endures to this day. Falun Gong may prove to have an equally long shelf life, but Falun Gong is not yet ten years old, and it would be injudicious to rush to a definitive judgement. It's certainly too soon, in our view, for Li to compare his movement to — let alone boast that it surpasses or supersedes — the rich traditions it draws so heavily upon.

As for the internal and global ramifications of Li's message, these are early days. China, as we shall see, is in the midst of profound upheaval, as it struggles to come to terms with twenty-first-century reality. Its greatest challenges — including its further responses to Li Hongzhi and Falun Gong — await, and no one can predict with any degree of certainty what may happen next week. We propose, in our final chapter, all manner of alternative scenarios, from which intrepid readers are invited to pick and choose.

For the moment, we hope that the results of our research will present Li Hongzhi and his creation in as fair and realistic a light as possible. In the end, we are not theologians, but simply a lawyer and two writers who became intrigued by Falun Gong and by the bewildering shadings of its several religious forebears, themselves shaped in the mists of China's past by very similar forces. This is a vast and intimidating canvas to draw upon, and we are surely guilty of numerous omissions and over-simplifications, having rushed in — as Hilaire Belloc put it — "where angels would fear to tread." But, in that perhaps foolhardy spirit, we have tried our best to give the world a well-rounded book on an exceptional man and an unparalleled spiritual movement.

Ian Adams

Riley Adams

Rocco Galati

October 2000

Prologue

*O*n an early spring morning in Toronto, the eastern sky is already awash with a pale and insubstantial light. As the cityscape changes from night to day like a slowly developing photograph, two women make their way through the almost deserted streets of a downtown neighbourhood. Except for the occasional exchange in Mandarin, they are companionably silent. Chen-yung, the mother, is in her sixties, and only recently arrived from mainland China. In common with many women her age, she speaks little English. Lan-shuan, her daughter, is half that age, and fluent in both languages. This daily walk is for them a pleasant ritual in itself, a time of preparation for the physical and spiritual exercises that await.

Soon, the pair arrive at Christie Pits, a former gravel yard transformed decades ago into a spacious and popular park. Here they're warmly greeted by twenty or so other men and women, the majority of whom are Chinese-Canadians. They have gathered in the early-morning hours because they are true believers in and eager converts to Falun Gong, which in its formative years came seemingly out of nowhere, exploding supernova-like to become the fastest-growing spiritual movement on the face of the earth.

The greetings over, the group spreads out to form a ragged half circle around Lan-shuan, who begins to lead them in a series of slow rhythmic exercises — a scene repeated as dawn breaks in thousands of parks and public places in cities from Hong Kong to Moscow, from Stockholm, Sweden, to Lesotho, South Africa.

But just as Lan-shuan is about to lead the group into a position known as holding-the-wheel-before-the-head, assuming the requisite "serene and peaceful countenance," three men in dark suits emerge from the shadows of a clump of maple trees. They identify themselves as members of the local Chinese consulate, and begin to denounce the practitioners as cultists and anti-Chinese fanatics. They also issue very specific warnings: "We know who you are; we know where you and your families come from in China. They will pay for what you are doing here." With that, they stride away.

The group understands that these are not idle threats. Ever since the spring of 1999, Falun Gong practitioners everywhere have been the objects of ceaseless and mounting repression on the part of the Chinese government. The warnings issued to Lan-shuan and her friends are repeated daily in cities around the world, wherever a Falun Gong group gathers and the Chinese government has an official presence. These threats are a distant echo of the far more extreme terror visited upon fellow practitioners in China itself, where the followers of Li Hongzhi and Falun Gong are now, as they have been for the past two years, arguably the most persecuted spiritual movement in the world.

1
One

The Rise of Falun Gong

*L*i Hongzhi is a strongly built man who stands over six feet tall, a "north easterner" from the city of Gongzhuling (formerly known as Gongzhuling Town of Huaide County) in the province of Jilin, not far from the Manchurian border.

According to Xinhua, China's state-run news agency, Li was born on July 7, 1952. His childhood and adolescence, depending on whom you believe, were either singularly mundane or filled with the most prodigious accomplishments. What seems indisputable is that he attended, between 1960 and 1969, the Zhujiang Road Elementary School, the Fourth Middle School, and the 48th Middle School in Changchun City, graduating with the equivalent of a North American high-school diploma at the age of seventeen.

But almost at once, we find ourselves embroiled in alternate versions of the truth. Li would later claim that at a very early age he became the sole disciple of a Buddhist master named Quan Jue, under whose tutelage he began to practise the "Buddhist

Law," attaining "cultivation of the Law at the age of eight" — in other words, at about the time he entered the Chinese equivalent of the first grade. Then, at age twelve, he was talent-spotted by a figure he refers to as "The Taoist Master Eight-Pole Immortal," who taught him "Taoist Gongfu."

A similar though not identical version, as offered by an official Falun Gong publication entitled *A Short Biography of Mr. Li Hongzhi*, adds that by means of these studies, Li "acquired such great supernatural powers as the abilities to move and position objects, control things using his thoughts, and make himself invisible . . . understand the truth about the universe, perceive deeply the human life, as well as see mankind's past and prophesy mankind's future."

Another story, also floated at various times by Li, concerns other, later studies, undertaken from 1972 to 1975 at the feet of someone identified as the "True Taoist," who taught the "Taoist Great Way." These were interspersed with, or followed by, sessions somewhere in the mountains with another unnamed Buddhist, who imparted knowledge of the "Great Law."

One-on-one spiritual instruction is a normal practice in the Chinese tradition. A Buddhist or Taoist teacher will quite often select a promising pupil and guide him in this way. Nonetheless, we wonder how such stringent and time-consuming activities could have been kept secret from friends and family members, none of whom have ever confirmed them. The stories also sound a bit too pat to be true. Li's claim that he was "chosen" by a series of teachers who secretly disclosed to him their lore echoes stories of the Buddha, who is said to have studied with two hermits famous for their mastery of meditative arts. The youthful Buddha succeeded in absorbing their techniques with astonishing speed, and the sages requested that he some day return to instruct them. One can see why Li would wish to associate himself with such auspicious events. Li's claims notwithstanding, the

Chinese government's investigators have determined that his classmates, teachers and neighbours all described him as an ordinary child. His grades were average, and his only marked talent was for playing the trumpet. Even his brother Li Donghui, ten years his junior, had no early intimation of future greatness. He recalls Hongzhi as "deeply introverted" and shy, but courageous at need. At one point, Li seems to have rescued another child from the town's river, then left the scene to escape the congratulations that were showered upon him by people who'd witnessed his heroism.

According to Donghui, Li's one abiding concern, fitting in an eldest son, was the care of his family (which also included two sisters, Jun Li and Ping Li), as his parents had separated after his siblings were born. Otherwise, Donghui described his brother, at this stage at least, as a quiet, humble person, "always studying on his own." The only sign that Hongzhi was given to meditative practices occurred when the two boys went bicycling together in the mountains, where Hongzhi would sit cross-legged and compose his thoughts, a regimen that was at the time officially forbidden by the state.

Li's activities upon graduating from school also appear to have been undistinguished. But to be fair, the late 1960s was not an era of unparalleled opportunities. Rather, these were the wretched middle years of the Cultural Revolution. Chairman Mao Zedong's desperate attempts to reimpose upon China the early ideals of the actual revolution that had brought him to power in 1949 had frozen the country in time. Show trials became a constant scourge. Some 3 million hapless Communist Party members were blacklisted, and an estimated 200,000 lost their lives. Most people kept their heads down and tried to stay out of the line of fire, hoping simply to survive from one day to the next.

So, too, did Li Hongzhi. Perhaps in order to better support

his family, he decided upon graduation to join the military and, given his aptitude for music, enrolled as a bandsman in the Red Army. Between 1970 and 1978 he played the trumpet at an agricultural collective, which would have granted him scant opportunity to wander off and study with diverse gurus.

Later, he performed a similar function with the Jilin Provincial Forest Police Unit. Xinhua, which later quizzed his immediate associates and superiors, described Li as an ordinary soldier, although somewhat "conceited." (He did seem to retain a fondness for meditational exercises. On at least one occasion, he was caught performing them instead of martial tunes, and was duly punished by having to attend a number of re-education classes.)

From 1978 until 1982, he worked as an "attendant" at a hotel attached to the forest police unit, before returning to civilian life and finding a job with the security department of the Changchun City Grain and Oil Company. Here he remained until 1991. His employers told the authorities that, as far as they could determine, he displayed an ignorance of exercises, laws, or "cultivation" of anything, but that he had attended community "qigong" classes in 1988.

Convinced they were on to something, the government investigators pursued this line of questioning, and unearthed evidence that Li had been attracted to the qigong craze that swept Chinese society in the mid-1980s. Qigong (pronounced chee-gong) is a regimen of physical exercises and breathing techniques. Its name refers to the quest for "qi," a sort of vital life force, and to the means by which one attempts to cultivate its power ("gong"). (Falun Gong suggests a comparable — Li would argue a nobler and far more complex — attempt to gain similar results by means of a falun, a metaphorical wheel.)

If Xinhua is to be believed, Li Hongzhi first began studying chan mi gong (a sub-system of qigong) with a master named

Li Weidong in 1988, but remained only briefly under his tute-lage. He then switched to jiu gong and ba gua gong (two other sub-systems), under the direction of another savant named Yu Guangsheng. Xinhua claims that Li took careful note of all the exercises involved, then mixed and matched them with a series of dance techniques he had picked up while visiting relatives in Thailand. Two of Li's first disciples, named Li Jingchao and Liu Yuqing, have supposedly claimed that Jingchao helped Li come up with the exercises, which were whipped into their final form a short month before Li made his first public appearance.

Religion in China

*W*e should take a moment here to describe the status of religion in China at the time that Li made this first appearance.

There is not, and never has been, any such thing in China as a separation of church and state. Nor, on the other hand, has there ever been an official state religion. If there had been one, it would have been some form of ancestor worship, Confucianism, or Taoism. It would not have been Buddhism, which was (by Chinese standards) a spiritual late-comer. Had the Nationalist forces won the Chinese Civil War, they would probably have institutionalized Confucianism. They didn't win; Mao's Communists did. Since then, it could be argued that Mao's per-sonality cult, the idea of no religion at all, or Communist ideology itself, has been the state-approved doctrine.

China's constitution, enacted in 1982, provides for freedom of religious belief, but this is a sham. China's Criminal Law states clearly that government officials who deprive citizens of their religious freedom may be sentenced to up to two years in prison, but there are no cases on record of anyone being so charged and punished.

At the moment, the government allows citizens to practise

five faiths — Buddhism, Taoism, Islam, Catholicism, or Protestantism — as long as they do so at state-controlled institutions that regulate their activities. But unofficial or "underground" churches of every variety proliferate and the persecution of them tends to ebb and flow, depending on the government's mood. It also varies from region to region. Tibet and Mongolia tend to be hotbeds of repression, because in these and other areas, religion is seen to be closely associated with the cultural and national identities of various ethnic groups, which must be kept in their place.

The government's current attitude, which involves increasing vigilance and equally increasing use of force, dates from 1994, when a new statute decreed that any place of religious activity had to register with the state and be supervised by an official, "patriotic" religious organization. In general, though, the preceding twenty years had seen an easing of state controls, coupled with a continuing resurgence of religious impulses. At the moment, according to a government white paper, there are more than 200 million religious adherents among China's 1.3 billion people. They represent a wide variety of practices and beliefs. Most would seem to profess Eastern faiths, but an estimated 42 million follow some form of Christianity. Many, as noted, are under a degree of duress, no matter what the constitution says.

This helps explain why Li never presented Falun Gong as a religion (which, as we will explain, it in fact is not). He wanted no part of government regulation and red tape. Rather, he termed it a "cultivation system" — or at most, a "spiritual belief system." This enabled him to avoid confrontation with the government.

The Early Voyage of Li Hongzhi

*L*i's debut took place in 1991, when the government had begun to show signs of relaxing its control over traditional religious activities, thus emboldening Li to take unpaid leave from the grain and oil company, journey to Beijing, and take the first step on his march to greatness.

His first audience was in a public hall and, by everyone's account, numbered roughly five hundred people, all of whom had turned out because of their interest in qigong. At this time, the woods were full of qigong schools, authorized by the government and banded together in a loose-knit organization called the Qigong Research Association of China. There were — as indicated above — hundreds of variations on the qigong theme, but all made some use of the same graceful movements, which are deeply rooted in thousands of years of Chinese culture. (Westerners who have visited China, or who have seen these exercises taking place in North American cities, tend to lump them together under the catch-all designation of "tai chi," which is geared to self-defence.) When Li arrived in Beijing, an estimated 50 million Chinese were more or less active qigong participants. They had seen it all before, because hundreds of would-be "qigong masters" had wrung just about every possible change out of the basic drill.

Qigong had fallen into official disfavour when Mao came to power, and was denounced as a lingering manifestation of the "ancient superstitious beliefs of Taoism and Buddhism." But it never went away, and it gradually resurfaced as the Cultural Revolution wore on. Just as gradually, the government began to change its tune. Whether or not they were superstitious, qigong exercises were indisputably Chinese; they therefore came to be viewed as politically correct, worthy of polite attention, if not outright devotion.

To be clear, qigong was sanctioned by the authorities only because of its practical benefits as a fitness regime. It might well lead to the holistic cultivation of both mind and body, but the government was looking for a direct pay-off. When people exercise regularly, they tend to be healthier, which takes pressure off the overburdened public health system. Thus, qigong was either left pretty much alone, or actively encouraged by the Communist Party, many of whose members also took part in qigong activities.

As noted, lots of self-appointed masters leapt on the qigong bandwagon, and bored their listeners stiff with theories of their own devising. Sometimes they overlaid a spiritual message, but qigong was not a religion. The members of Li's first modest audience weren't looking for or anticipating another saviour or guru. They'd come to hear him out of curiosity, but were electrified by his lecture. By all accounts, Li was a natural. He spoke fluently and easily, demonstrating his five simple sets of exercises, and referring only occasionally to a few notes written on scraps of paper.

If Li hadn't succeeded that day, he might have disappeared, never to be heard from again, like a special guest or warm-up act who didn't click with the crowd. But Li clicked in some way that we can only guess at. Many of the people who heard his speech would certainly have been far better educated and more sophisticated than he. Some, as we shall see, were prominent members of the Communist Party. In short, they weren't an easy sell, and we can only marvel at Li's achievement. Here was a basically private man, on the verge of turning forty, who had spent his life as an obscure and anonymous functionary. Whether or not he was actually instructed by Eight-Pole Masters is immaterial. He had obviously read deeply and studied widely in order to assemble his own version of material that everybody else had already wrung dry — a version that at once commanded the attention of a blasé and jaded audience.

All of this is wildly improbable, but not without precedent. Very few Chinese had heard of the Buddha before he crossed the border from northern India, and the fabled Confucius was a police chief in his home state. The weary self-help cliché is quite true: ordinary people are capable of extraordinary things, and Li accomplished something extraordinary that day. After his presentation ended, the audience crowded around him, unwilling to let him go. Immediately, many people offered to aid him in his work. Among them was his brother Donghui, who would shortly leave his job as a Communist Party official specializing in international trade commissions and begin to labour full time on Li's behalf. "It really wasn't until 1991 that I came to see all the things that he had brought together to create Falun Gong," Donghui told us. "Master Li was the right man in the right place at the right time. But more than that, he had the right stuff." (Note that Donghui refers to his brother as "Master," the worshipful title bestowed upon Li by his disciples.)

In any case, word of Li's speech travelled fast, far, and wide, prompting the organizers of the first event to invite him back a few weeks later. This time, he drew several thousand people. Videos of these early gatherings reveal that he usually wore an open-necked shirt under a suit jacket; his expression was either serene or half-smiling. He started off slowly, but soon began to build, becoming more animated as he went along and peppering the rapid-fire delivery of his rambling lectures with the catchphrase exhortation, "Think about it, everyone." Plainly, everyone thought about it. After his third and fourth appearances, there were no halls large enough to contain the tens of thousands who wanted to hear his message.

Falun Gong as Belief

*L*i's message should be summarized here, but we will return to it in greater detail, and with considerably more critical analysis, in Chapter Three. We will attempt to explain each term as it first appears, but be warned that some words and phrases defy direct translation. The idea of "practitioners" as opposed to believers, adherents, or followers is easy to grasp, and quite accurate, in that Falun Gong requires people to perform or practise various exercises. But "cultivation," for example, is more elusive, even though it's part of an ancient tradition. Buddhists and believers in other faiths speak of it also. It's best thought of as a mixture of pursuit, questing, improvement, examination, realization, and attainment.

Bear in mind that all religions (or belief systems) are deeply personal matters of faith, difficult to articulate and by nature and definition impossible to prove. East and West are one in this regard; the niceties of Roman Catholic dogma, to cite a single example, would strike many disinterested parties as ridiculous. Much of what Li talks about, and what his followers profess to believe, simply cannot be shoehorned into a form that's readily accessible to most Western readers. Some of it, try as we may to explain it, will be as meaningless to non-believers as would a discussion of the final moves of a chess game between grand masters to someone who'd received only a basic grounding in the rules and moves, but had never played the game.

From the start, Li was throwing everything he could think of into the Falun Gong mix. This is not a criticism. China's religious history has always been marked by remembering and borrowing from the past, and by the hope that various parts might be brought together to form a whole. In the sixth century, a scholar named Li Shiqian remarked that Buddhism was the sun, Taoism the moon, and Confucianism the five planets. During the Yuan and Ming dynasties — that is, from the thirteenth to the seventeenth centuries — attempts were made to merge these three systems into something best described as neo-Confucianism. From time to time, Buddhism and Taoism in particular became so cross-pollinated as to be almost indistinguishable.

Li used these facts to his advantage; he realized that most of his listeners were at least partially aware of what had gone before. Though long suppressed, the three great strands had never been totally forgotten. Whichever one his listeners favoured or dimly remembered, he could offer them a piece of it, wrapped up in a fresh package. While very careful to avoid positing himself as a religious leader, he laid claim to a great deal of territory, nudging the boundaries of what was advisable or permissible for a garden-variety qigong master to say. Anything that struck a familiar chord was appropriated as grist for Falun Gong's mill. For example, the hand gestures that accompanied Li's exercises were especially attractive and exciting to a Chinese audience because of their close resemblance to the outlawed Tibetan Buddhist magical signs known as mudras. Li was, if nothing else, a consummate synthesizer.

He also knew how to get the word out. Very soon, his early speeches were revised and amplified into a wide-ranging system. Exactly how this was done remains obscure. Li himself may have written or dictated the material or, at least at first, his lecture notes and exercise instructions may have been expanded and written down by his disciples, then authorized by him. Later still, his system was compiled into two books: *China Falun Gong* and *Zhuan Falun*. Their contents comprise the sacred texts.

Li teaches, and his followers believe, that Falun Gong constitutes an advanced system of cultivating both body and mind, with the final aim of attempting to reach "consummation" during one's lifetime. Consummation refers to an ascension beyond this life to one's "true essence." It also entails enlightenment —

which, once achieved, enables a person to perceive the truth of the cosmos. Consummation and enlightenment can be attained only if one practises, follows, and lives out "three universal truths": Zhen (pronounced jhun and meaning truth), Shan (meaning benevolence or compassion), and Ren (meaning forbearance or endurance).

Of these attributes, Li considers Ren to be by far the most important. Only by enduring life's hardships and tribulations and exercising forbearance (an idea rather like the Christian notion of turning the other cheek, but more proactive and not to be confused with simple acceptance or toleration) can practitioners succeed in converting karma (a "black" or undesirable substance accumulated during their past and present lifetimes) into de (pronounced duh — a white, milky substance). This enables them to atone for past and present transgressions, and to cultivate their xinxing (pronounced sheen-shing, and meaning "mind and heart" or one's "true nature"). An enhanced xinxing in turn increases practitioners' "cultivation energy" and "energy potency" — an ongoing process that starts off with, but does not depend on, Falun Gong's exercises.

The teachings of Falun Dafa begin with the premise that the true essence of any human being is good. Further, human beings are not created on earth (the basest and crudest form of existence in the cosmos), but at a higher level. That level is a person's true essence. On earth, everyone inhabits a body of flesh, which is part of a person's benti (pronounced bun-tee), an entity that also includes a person's other bodies as they are manifested in different dimensions. These exist simultaneously with the earthly body, but remain invisible until cultivation opens the "third" or "celestial" eye, allowing a practitioner to see things in other spaces — and, for that matter, to see through the human body as clearly as an x-ray machine in order to pinpoint illness and psychological problems.

The cultivation process also involves the figurative insertion of a falun (or wheel) into a practitioner's abdomen. The falun, according to Li, is an intelligent entity, whose sentience can be increased by means of meditation. It has discovered the secret of perpetual motion. It rotates incessantly in both directions, moving clockwise to absorb energy from the cosmos, and counter-clockwise to release it, offering "salvation to all life" and "rectifying abnormal states." This cosmic connection takes place because the falun's rotation is synchronized with that of the universe. Indeed, it represents the universe in miniature. As practitioners cultivate their xinxings, the wheel rotates more "fervently," energy is more efficiently absorbed and distributed, and the body is emptied of disease and immoral behaviour — just as, when the clarity of the third eye increases, practitioners can focus on higher planes of consciousness.

On close inspection, the falun seems to be Li's variation on such concepts as the Taoist belief in yin and yang (two opposite and mutually exclusive though interdependent forces) and the Buddhist teachings known collectively as dharma (release from suffering on the wheel of eternal becoming). But the falun is not the only entity that Li pledges to insert into practitioners' mortal frames. He also (figuratively) endows the faithful with "law bodies," a sort of cross between guardian angels and all-purpose vaccines.

Li maintains that the cultivation of one's xinxing involves giving up all "attachments" or obsessive desires. Practitioners should therefore "make light of and disregard such things as personal fame and gain." This does not mean, however, that they must turn their backs on worldly possessions or spurn everyday endeavours. Rather, they're expected to live and function in the world, but to avoid being driven by its trappings. Nor is there a prohibition against wealth, as long as it's not obtained or used in ways that contradict universal principles.

All this, as noted, begins with the exercises, which serve three purposes. First, they are themselves a form of forbearance. While simple, they demand endurance both in execution and in the discipline required for their daily repetition. They also assist in conditioning the body, improving concentration, and maintaining the will to cultivate, and augmenting the components of, one's xinxing. They are important because they start a practitioner off on the path to cultivation, but they are not the crux of Li's system. Nor are they to be confused with the outwardly similar exercises found in tai chi, yoga, or any other qigong system whose ultimate objective is the attainment of simple qi. The farther a practitioner advances, the less relevant the exercises become to the task of attaining the higher goals of cultivation energy and eventual enlightenment.

The remainder of Li's original message was actually quite straightforward: take care of yourself and your family, respect your neighbours, choose not to hate your enemies, abjure violence, and in general strive to be a better person. All practitioners were expected to abstain from smoking, drinking, and pre- or extramarital sex. (Li's views on sex are straight-laced. He abhors homosexuality, deeming it to be a vice on par with murder and drug abuse.)

Take faluns and law bodies out of the mix, and the basic teachings are surprisingly simple. They also offer the important advantage of speed. Falun Gong is user-friendly — so much so that doubting skeptics have labelled it McBuddhism, or Buddhism Lite. Li's message is enlightenment while you wait, served up quickly and (by Eastern standards) informally. You won't have to spend years of contemplation in caves or on mountaintops, because by Lecture Four in his series of ten ninety-minute cassettes, you'll be "purified" in body, mind, and soul — but only if you order from Li's menu. Then, when enlightenment dawns, you'll be ready to press on to even higher levels of cultivation, allowing you (again, given the right attitude) to achieve "supernatural" powers of perception and healing.

Master Li — "Evil Cult Leader" or Spiritual Leader?

*P*erhaps, having offered this preliminary description of Li's teachings and his relationship with his practitioners, we ought to confront his alleged status as a cult leader. At first glance, he seems to qualify to some degree, but this is largely a case of guilt by association. Self-proclaimed prophets with extravagant views always inspire snap judgements and knee-jerk reactions — usually from self-appointed "cult-watching groups" who display their own biases in the process. In fact, it could be said that a cult is just a mainstream religion that hasn't been around for 2,000 years. Think of how the Romans must have looked upon an itinerant preacher from Galilee with his own brand of over-the-top rhetoric and a paltry dozen disciples.

When we consider that cult leaders are traditionally concerned with fleecing their followers at every turn, Li doesn't seem to qualify. The Chinese government alleges that, while resident in China, he profited by his activities — not in itself a crime. He has never denied that his writings and other materials are his source of income. Investigations elsewhere have unearthed few signs that Li, his family, or Falun Gong's inner circle are rolling in wealth, apart from a donated house (which we'll encounter in Chapter Two) that he apparently refused to accept or occupy.

There are no patents pending on the celestial eye, and no membership fees in Falun Gong. No one seems to demand money from practitioners, who (at least in China) don't have all that much to begin with. Li's books and cassette tapes are available worldwide for modest sums, and many materials can be downloaded from the Internet for free. Participation in Falun

Gong activities seems to be entirely voluntary. No one is asked or compelled to abandon family, friends, and work. On the contrary, Li continues to encourage believers to lead a normal social and working life, and above all, to avoid politics. He exhorts practitioners to be model citizens, no matter where, and under what kind of government, they live.

No one is hustled off to remote retreats and charged ever-mounting sums for layers or tiers of instruction. No one is directed to importune travellers in airports or seek converts door to door. There is no formal initiation. All you have to do, if you wish to practise, is show up at a local park one morning, join in the exercises, and take part in the discussion session. Perhaps you'll be asked if you want to buy a book or tape, but free printouts are usually available. Although someone will be appointed to lead group members through their exercises, Falun Gong has no clergy and no churches. By one widely accepted definition, it's not a religion, because there is no god involved. At least in theory, one can be both a Falun Gong practitioner and a worshipping Christian, Muslim, or Jew.

The Chinese government keeps trying to pin an "evil cult" label on the Falun Gong, in part because it hopes to scrape a raw nerve in the West, particularly in the United States. Americans have every right to be edgy about weirdos of every stripe, having weathered such personalities and entities as the Manson Family, Jim Jones and Jonestown, David Koresh, the organizers of Heaven's Gate and the Solar Temple, Hare Krishna, the Reverend Moon, the Bhagwan Rajneesh, and hundreds more. But Americans in particular remain unconvinced that Li is a cult leader. Westerners might think Li a touch odd if they bumped into his writings unawares, but he has not yet been cast as anything approaching a demonic figure. Despite the Chinese government's incessant propaganda campaign, even the most skeptical media coverage of Falun Gong's activities goes only so far as to use the terms "sect" or "quasi-religious group." Even the U.S. State Department (which admittedly has its own axe to grind, having granted Li both asylum and a Green Card) takes care to refer always to Falun Gong as a "spiritual movement."

All that having been said, it must be added that Li almost certainly has exhorted or directed his followers in China to put themselves in harm's way, with — as we shall see — painful and sometimes fatal results. They, at least, must be assumed to be in large part under his sway. He also preaches the imminence of apocalypse (a stock indication of cultism), and refers explicitly to the present day as "the final period of Last Havoc." He seems to match several of the criteria set out by the investigative writer Robert Jay Lifton, who notes in *Destroying the World to Save It* that new religions are typically marked by leaders who embody "everything and nothing." The "everything" acknowledges "the guru's creation of his own group and its belief system, as well as his sustained control over it," while the "nothing" gives him ample opportunity to charge off in new directions at need. This sounds a lot like Li.

Lifton also notes that cult leaders are always products of a particular historical moment, representing "a specific time and place, even as they draw upon ancient psychological and theo-logical themes." This is an exact description of Li's initial rise within China. Lifton goes on to point out that both cult leaders and their followers are "psychologically unmoored" — a state that allows a leader to improvise both his theology and his personal life, becoming "a floating guru." Again, this nicely encapsulates Li's activities since he fled to, and disappeared in, the United States.

The trouble is that Lifton is talking specifically about a demonstrably violent and evil cult, the Japanese Aum Shrinrykio, which in 1995 released a deadly nerve gas aboard the Tokyo subway. There may well be elements of cultism in Li's approach, especially his most recent behaviour, and in the unquestioning acceptance of his message by his followers, but we must be extremely wary of imposing a convenient all-purpose template. Instead, we must proceed slowly, feature by feature, in an attempt to come to grips with the confusing and, in many particulars, contradictory realities of Li and Falun Gong.

Building a Movement

The reasons behind Li's remarkable initial success are equally complex. In brief, more than four decades of Chinese Communism had left the world's most populated country starved for a spiritual dimension to life, and Li emerged as the man who could feed this hunger. Communism had failed to deliver its promised panacea, and Red Capitalism seemed unlikely to do much better. People were searching for a new way — a quest not limited to the suffering underclasses. Their traditional forms of spiritual expression barred by the government, they turned to Li, who would become the conduit through which the Chinese could rediscover their philosophical and religious inheritance, a rich legacy buried, neglected, and prohibited for so long. Li's teachings filled a vacuum at a time when people were desperate for something, anything, to turn to. As Ye Hao, a former senior Party member now living in self-imposed exile, told us: "For years nobody had really believed in the official 'religion,' the dogma of the Communist Party. They only gave lip service to it, because this was necessary in order for them to survive." If this is so, any charismatic figure would have served to capture the people's attention, and Li was the right man in the right place with an approximation of the right stuff.

But Li and his disciples also worked tirelessly to promote the spread of Falun Gong. As noted, Li first joined, but later withdrew from, the legally sanctioned qigong association. While under its umbrella, he assiduously cultivated influential members of the Communist Party, many of whom became practitioners. At this time, he received numerous official accolades for his work. In December 1993, for example, he was presented (at a gathering called the Oriental Health Expo) with a plaque proclaiming him as "Qigong Master Most Acclaimed by the Masses," and was a featured guest at events sponsored by the ministries of Public Security and Central Propaganda.

Meanwhile, his fame had spread apace. He could not appear in public without attracting huge crowds that would halt traffic for blocks. His brother Donghui described to us how the police would come to investigate the cause of the disturbance, with a view to sending gawkers packing. "Then they would find out it was Master Li. They would jump to help him, escorting him through the crowds, telling him how proud they were to meet him and confiding in him that they were practitioners and that everyone in their families followed Falun Dafa."

Next, having severed connections with the qigong association, Li established the Beijing-based Research Society of Falun Dafa, and appointed himself its president. He simultaneously embarked on a burst of activity that renders invalid his later protestations that he had "no organizational structure." On the contrary, Falun Gong was comprehensively organized from top to bottom, and soon included thirty-nine "master stations" located in major centres, 1,900 "branch stations" in smaller cities and towns, and more than 2,800 "group exercise areas" where Falun Gong practitioners could regularly gather.

The master stations, as their name implies, were responsible for organizing large-scale activities with a view to "expanding the teachings" and enabling interested parties to "understand the way of practice." They also hosted a number of periodic "celebrations" and "commemorations," stocked Li's books, cassettes, and video tapes, attempted to drum up good publicity, and strove to dampen adverse comment. All of this paid off almost at once. Li may not have been rolling in wealth, but he was definitely comfortable (and publicity conscious) enough to donate the equivalent of $5,000 U.S. to a fund created to benefit officers in the Public Security Bureau who'd been injured by criminals in the line of duty. He also, on several occasions, seems to have provided free medical treatment to them and to other bureau personnel.

Another reason for Li's out-of-the-gate success is very basic indeed: his early converts did much of his work for him. To grasp how this happened so rapidly, we have only to remember the overriding importance of family in Chinese society — a basically Confucian idea. Word travels more quickly in China than Westerners can imagine; it's a sort of super-domino effect that moves through 1.3 billion people. One day, a woman learns of Li's teachings and attends a cultivation session. She feels renewed, invigorated, and morally recharged. She informs a cousin of this happy circumstance, and he in turn informs two brothers, each of whom tells an uncle. Almost at once, news of Li's teachings crackles over a thousand telephone lines. If the first audience in a given city consists of uncommitted walk-ins, the next gathering will be so well attended that it's standing room only in a hastily rented first-floor office space, with the crowd spilling out onto the dimly lit street. A year later, only a soccer stadium will suffice to seat the supporters intent on hearing Li's teachings in person.

By September 1994, however, signs began to emerge that Li had even greater goals in mind. At this time, he changed his birth date and re-registered his identity card. His actual birth date, as noted, was almost certainly July 7, 1952. Now, he claimed to have been born on May 13, 1951. According to his detractors, this was because the Buddha was said to have been born on that day — the eighth day of the fourth month of China's lunar calendar. When questioned by Western reporters, Li explained that the new date was correct, and that he merely wanted to straighten out a bureaucratic blunder. But in the East, where every major religion espouses reincarnation as a fundamental tenet, the message was loud and clear. According to the Chinese government, Li wished to proclaim himself the reincarnation of the Buddha, in keeping with his long-term aspiration — to become a prophet who would supplant and supersede the Buddha in the eyes of the faithful.

The Buddha, who died in his eighties, supposedly as a result of eating bad pork, was at least graceful enough to remain in one place, concerned to the end with his followers' condition. But in 1997, Li — who had meanwhile married and had two children — abruptly headed with his family for the United States. (Later, his mother and one sister would join him there; his second sister now lives in southeast Asia.) No convincing explanation for his departure has ever been put forward. Neither he, his organization, nor his followers were at the time under extreme duress. He faced, as far as we can determine, no imminent peril, nor would one arise for almost two years. This was not his first trip to America. He appears to have made at least one previous visit in 1996, but did not at that time obtain (although he may have applied for) a Green Card. He went, initially at least, to New York City, where he expressed delight to be able to walk about the streets of Chinatown. Then, two years later, he dropped mysteriously — perhaps permanently — out of sight.

Throughout the period before his disappearance, Li and his closest disciples travelled the world to establish Falun Dafa groups in various major cities. But his departure did not slow the growth of Falun Gong in China. In early 1999, according to the Chinese authorities' own estimates, there were approximately 100 million practitioners — double the membership of the Communist Party itself. This figure was arrived at by the Public Security Bureau, which instructed every known qigong group and association to ask its members whether they were first and foremost adherents of Falun Gong. Presumably, since the government had yet to launch its repression in earnest, and they could answer without fear of reprisal, the associations told the truth. "With that many people," said Ye Hao, the former Public Security Bureau executive, "you can run the country."

At the beginning of the Chinese New Year of 1999, Li Hongzhi and Falun Gong had much to celebrate. It was a Year of the Rabbit in the lunar calendar, which begins on February 6. Years of the Rabbit are traditionally peaceful and productive, the only pitfall being that matters may become a trifle sentimental. And all the other omens were positive indeed.

In China, millions of converts continued to flock to Li's banner, without facing much in the way of official disapproval. True, there had been isolated incidents, but they had come and gone, shrugged off as unfortunate misunderstandings. Thousands of Falun Gong's training and study centres dotted the mainland; every city and town awoke to the familiar sight of practitioners going about their early-morning exercises. Li's publisher in Hong Kong (since closed by the authorities) worked overtime to meet an ever-increasing worldwide demand, churning out millions of copies of his books in many different languages. Despite his continued absence, the movement seemed to be on automatic pilot. The search for qi, by means of numerous qigong systems, was deemed chic, an "in" activity among the highest levels of Chinese society. Most important, Falun Gong had been more or less overtly embraced in senior governmental and bureaucratic circles. "When we practised in different cities," remembers Ye Hao, "I'd look around me, and all I could see were fellow Party members." With visible support emanating from the corridors of power, no harm could befall.

As a Buddhist would say, "everything was empty and full of light," meaning that for Li and Falun Gong the future was bright and limitless. All was possible, and no serious problems lay ahead. Li Hongzhi's cup overflowed with promise. But eight weeks later it would suddenly and violently shatter.

Two

The Long Night
of Falun Gong

*O*n April 25, 1999, ten thousand Falun Gong practitioners mounted a silent and ghostly protest outside Beijing's Zhongnanhai Communist Party headquarters, best described as a Chinese Kremlin. They had assembled overnight, quietly filling the sidewalks around the building. At first, they stood shoulder to shoulder, then sat, legs crossed in the "lotus" position, facing out into the street in ranks as many as eight deep.

They had a legal right to do so under the terms of China's constitution, which permits every citizen to "appeal" any perceived injustice. Usually, such appeals are presented at police stations and court houses. The Zhongnanhai protesters' aims were twofold: to request the release of fellow practitioners who'd been arrested during previous demonstrations, and to request that the government recognize Falun Gong as an independent, state-sanctioned organization. They would succeed only in the first of these aims, and only briefly, as we shall see. But this assembly was peaceful and for the most part without incident.

Unable to meet with senior government officials, the practitioners dispersed and went back home, although many would return over the course of the next several days. By the time this protest — or more accurately, this series of protests — ended, something like 30,000 people would have gathered outside the Zhongnanhai and in the adjacent Tiananmen Square.

The police were totally unprepared for the scale of this demonstration (which may explain why they didn't respond with massive arrests) and irked because they had not known for sure that it was about to occur. They had been gearing up for all sorts of trouble, but were looking too far down the line, to the tenth anniversary of the Tiananmen Square massacre, which took place on June 4, 1989. That such a massive protest could take place without the authorities getting wind of it, especially given their vast and usually efficient network of paid informers, was deeply troubling. How did Falun Gong, which had persisted (and would continue to persist) in claiming that it had no organization to speak of, manage to pull off such an obviously well-coordinated challenge to the Party at its seat of power? Both government and Party suffered an immediate loss of face, and felt threatened as seldom before.

That loss of face was doubly hard to bear because it was international. The Zhongnanhai protest, simply because of its critical mass, became front-page news around the world, increasing the Chinese government's unease. As a rule, the West receives very little in-depth reporting on Chinese events — stories that are unauthorized by the state and go beyond cursory, isolated snapshots. And in this case, much of the live coverage and post-demonstration commentary was superficial, because few media were in a position to provide any sort of context for readers and television viewers. Still, the sight of thousands of protesters, no matter who they were or what they were up to, qualified as eminently newsworthy, and obviously posed some sort of threat to the Party's hold on the nation.

While the authorities were taken aback by the size of the Zhongnanhai demonstration, they had had ample evidence that it was in the wind. The police had been engaged for quite some time in scattered and relatively minor confrontations with Falun Gong. In May 1998, according to the Hong Kong–based Centre for Human Rights and Democracy in China, the police claimed that key members of "the master station in Beijing of the Research Society of Falun Dafa" had incited more than a thousand practitioners to "besiege" the local state-run television station because it had aired a program that criticized Falun Gong. (The police also claimed that one "key member" had been deposed by his fellows because he failed to display sufficient enthusiasm for this activity.)

More recently, on April 23, 1999, a small gathering of prac-titioners at Tianjin Normal University had suddenly escalated into a mass protest that engulfed the campus and involved 6,000 demonstrators. That same day, another group of practitioners had held a silent dawn vigil in Tiananmen Square. This gathering was spurred by the arrest a few days earlier of fellow practitioners in the nearby port city of Tianjin who had surrounded the offices of a state-run magazine that had run an article describing Falun Gong as "fraudulent and dangerous." That incident ended, according to Zhang Erping, the New York–based disciple, when "the police came and drove them away with great force, arresting many people." These were the arrests that the Zhongnanhai pro-testers were petitioning to have addressed.

Not surprisingly, the Zhongnanhai demonstration led to charges on the part of the government that Li Hongzhi had "master-minded" the gathering from abroad. These charges were not without substance, since on the morning of April 24, many

Falun Gong practising sites in Beijing had received by both fax and e-mail a notice urging them to stage "collective practising" outside the Zhongnanhai the next day. But at about this point, the plot began to thicken.

On April 30, during a telephone interview with a Shanghai-based reporter for the *Wall Street Journal*, Li denied that he had instigated the protest, stating that he in fact knew nothing about it. On May 2, he turned up in Sydney, Australia, where he repeated his previous claim — adding that, on the day of the Zhongnanhai demonstration, he was en route to Australia from the United States, and first learned about the protest upon arrival in Brisbane.

These denials would soon be claimed by the Chinese government to be improbable. The Chinese government is capable of all sorts of falsehoods, but in this case it managed to compile a highly detailed and reasonably convincing body of evidence that contradicts Li's assertions.

According to the Public Security Bureau, Li actually arrived in Beijing from the United States on the afternoon of April 22 aboard Northwest Airlines — the first time since 1997 he had set foot on Chinese soil. He represented himself as a businessman, and carried a U.S. re-entry visa. While he was in Beijing, the disturbance broke out at Tianjin Normal University, and the first protest took place in Tiananmen Square. Then, on the afternoon of April 24, a day before the gathering at the Zhongnanhai, he left the country for Hong Kong aboard China International Airways, and continued to Brisbane aboard Cathay Pacific Airways on the evening of April 27.

In support of these claims, the police produced Li's arrival and departure cards, both personally filled out and signed by him. This seems to confirm, if nothing else, that they had him under strict surveillance, and were aware of his every move — but two questions remain. Why, given that he was being watched, did the authorities fail to intercept and detain him? And more important, what was he doing so close to the scene of the action?

No definitive answer to either question has yet emerged, but one possible scenario goes as follows. Li arrived in Beijing in anticipation of some momentous event; nothing else would have drawn him back to China. He fled because he realized that his plans had gone awry. Perhaps he had believed that the Tiananmen and Zhongnanhai protests would result in an offer of rapprochement on the part of the government, a sign that some form of recognition of Falun Gong's legitimacy was at hand. At that point, Li, waiting in the wings, would have stepped forward to make a grand reappearance, timed perhaps to coincide with May 13, the Buddha's birthday.

Unfortunately, we'll never know what was in Li's mind. His disciples are fuzzy and evasive when pressed for details on these crucial events. The idea of a government turn-around, in which it would welcome Li back with open arms, seems far-fetched, although Ye Hao maintains that in the early spring of 1999, "there seemed to be a strong possibility of accommodation on the part of the government to this new phenomenon. There were many talks between the leadership of Falun Gong and senior government ministers. We were about to work out something." Exactly what took place during these behind-the-scenes gatherings is unclear, but Ye states that he and an airforce general named Li Zang had previously made applications to the government at about this time, seeking permanent legal status for Falun Gong as a spiritual organization.

If so, it's possible that Li Hongzhi seriously underestimated his main adversary — President Jiang Zemin.

President Jiang — Force or Figurehead?

Jiang, the hand-picked successor of Deng Xiaoping, was easy to underestimate. He was widely considered to be a stand-in patsy for his mentor. While the mayor of Shanghai, he had been nicknamed "The Flowerpot" — an ineffectual adornment to the Party who spent his time cutting ribbons and giving boring speeches.

Popular wisdom held that Deng had chosen Jiang to succeed him in 1997 because he believed that an "outsider" could rule more easily, and could continue his program of economic reforms without being too liberal, which would cause the country to unravel. Such a leader could not be compromised by connections to the old guard. Jiang, in Deng's view, fit the bill. Alone among China's Communist leaders, Jiang had not fought in, or indeed played any part in, the revolution. Rather, he had worked in a factory, attended college in Moscow, and worked as an engineer, specializing in mass production technology. Over the years, he had climbed quietly and steadily through the Party ranks, but was generally looked upon as faceless and devoid of any real broad-based support.

This impression was incorrect. Jiang's mentor Deng repeatedly stated that "a leader cannot rule without a core." Jiang had taken this maxim to heart, and had worked incessantly behind the scenes to develop his own "core" power group.

In today's China, power derives mainly from two sources: the state bureaucracy and the perceived legitimacy of the ruler. The latter attribute, along with an attendant "cult of personality," has persisted in Chinese political culture since Confucian times. In bygone centuries, an emperor enjoyed divine privilege — that is, supreme legitimacy — only until rebellion, plague, war, or famine broke out. On those occasions, he had to deal with harsh reality. His powers were sweeping, but his position was, in fact, precarious. Calamities were considered to be tests imposed by the gods. If a leader responded to them quickly and efficiently, his legitimacy was confirmed. If not, the people could and did cast him out.

Aware that he had to start from scratch to consolidate his power, Jiang first looked to the state bureaucracy. Here he was on reassuringly familiar ground. He'd spent many years observing the system, and knew exactly what to do.

China is governed on a day-to-day basis by a bureaucratic system divided into four major functional areas known as "kou." These areas are Party affairs, government work, state security, and foreign affairs. Each kou also includes a number of sub-kou. For example, state security is divided into the military, and political and legal affairs. The entire apparatus is based not on merit but on political appointment. Whoever controls the levers of patronage controls the system and ensures a binding form of loyalty.

Jiang's efforts in this regard were prodigious, driven by a work ethic that would have excited the envy of the most hard-driving Western business executive. For example, between 1982 and 1985, he was simultaneously vice-chairman and secretary-general of the State Import-Export Administration Committee; first vice-minister and deputy secretary of the Party core group; and minister and secretary of the Ministry of Electronic Industry.

Working from the bottom up, he systematically replaced department heads until he'd transformed and in effect "owned" the ministries he'd targeted. By these means, he soon became general secretary of the Communist Party of China's Central Committee, chairman of its Central Military Commission, and a member of both the Standing Committee of its Political Bureau and its Central Committee, Military State. No modern Chinese leader had so rapidly and effectively centralized so much power unto himself.

Key to this power grab were the Chinese security and military services, which from the outset were Jiang's primary focus. When he was the mayor of Shanghai, he had assiduously catered to the needs of visiting heads of government (Shanghai has always been a favourite vacation spot for government executives and was indeed where Jiang cemented his relationship with Deng). Jiang now began to seek out the most powerful figures in the Chinese armed forces. He moved quickly to gain control of the security area, reshaping the Provincial Armed Police (PAP) into an FBI-like force that could control civil disorder without having to resort to the overwhelming firepower of the People's Liberation Army (PLA). He further ensured the loyalty of the PAP by staffing it with officers and men who had been demobilized from the PLA and were now unemployed. They were thus grateful and loyal to him beyond question.

From the very beginning of Jiang's tenure, China's most senior generals were given increased roles in civilian affairs. Jiang changed the Party's constitution, guaranteeing them seats in the seven-man ruling Politburo. He also promoted a number of more junior officers to the rank of general, an adept move that consolidated his support at the top.

He had started to clean house as long ago as 1989, just after the massacre of student demonstrators in Tiananmen Square. At that time, he made wholesale changes in both the military and the PLA, removing anyone who had displayed support of or sympathy towards the students' protest and putting in place his own men. By 1996, all seven of China's Military Regional Commanders were in some way beholden to him for their position. They repaid him by actively promoting a Jiang Zemin personality cult within the military ranks. No leader could have wished for a more influential and trustworthy core group.

It only remained for Jiang to demonstrate to the people at large that he had the requisite charisma to rule, despite his lack of an heroic and valiant role in the revolution. To assure a more broadly based personality cult, there had to be a major crisis, a suitable adversary against which he could move decisively, thus establishing his perceived legitimacy to govern.

Falun Gong suited Jiang's purpose admirably. Li and his disciples, who had somehow managed to command the allegiance of 100 million practitioners — an ominous figure, the more you thought about it — were seen by Jiang as both a tangible threat and a timely political gift. They had, for the most part, escaped censure until now, but no longer. Exercising in parks was one thing — rallying outside the Zhongnanhai, another. These latest demonstrations posed a direct challenge to Jiang's ability to rule, and might, if he allowed them to go unchecked, encourage other groups and organizations to stir up trouble of their own.

Jiang felt equal to the task at hand. Not only was he ready and waiting for the Falun Gong practitioners, he needed them. Now he would crush them without mercy. If their subjugation took place within view of television cameras, so much the better. In the words of an old Chinese saying, "To scare a monkey, you must kill a chicken." Jiang was determined to teach Falun Gong a lesson, and his message would be delivered forcefully and unmistakably from one end of China to the other, and to the world beyond.

Jiang's confrontations were not limited to Falun Gong. Shortly before the Zhongnanhai protest, authorities had targeted the Chinese Democratic Party (CDP). Three of its leaders were sentenced to lengthy prison terms in December 1998. Later, dozens of CDP members were arrested in a widening crackdown, and more of its leaders were convicted of subversion and sentenced to long prison terms in closed trials that flagrantly violated due process of law.

As well, throughout the winter of 1998, many unapproved religious groups, including underground Catholic and Protestant congregations, had continued to experience varying degrees of interference and repression. Services were disrupted, and church leaders were harassed, fined, detained, beaten, and tortured.

All of this was a countdown to the anniversary of the Tiananmen Square massacre, which loomed large in Jiang's mind. He believed that any number of protests might be timed to commemorate this event — a realistic expectation, since widespread resentment still smoulders against that dark chapter in China's history — but didn't know from which direction the protests would come. So, just to be on the safe side, security forces had begun to move systematically against political dissidents all across the country as the anniversary date drew closer, detaining and formally arresting scores of activists.

It is a wonder that Falun Gong, for the most part, escaped this warm-up purge. But its turn would no doubt have come, even if thousands of practitioners hadn't assembled, almost certainly at Li's direction, at the university campus, in Tiananmen Square, and then, as the final straw, outside the Zhongnanhai.

After the initial shock of that gathering, however, Jiang's retribution was somewhat slow in coming. Having denounced Li, he bided his time, and a brief lull ensued, while various highly placed members of the government attempted to calm things down. Their aim was to broker some sort of peaceful co-existence between the Communist Party and Falun Gong. All were prominent members of Falun Gong, and all believed — erroneously, as events would prove — that they could encourage both sides to reach a workable compromise. Among these participants were the airforce general Li Zang and another Security Bureau member named Li Xiajin.

Another close disciple, Ye Hao, by this time living outside China, felt uniquely suited to play the role of advisor. (Fearing a midnight visit from members of his former organization, Ye has asked us not to reveal his whereabouts. So, by the way, have several other disciples, including Li's brother, Li Donghui, and we have been careful to comply with their requests.) Ye had been present at Li Hongzhi's first speech in Beijing in 1991, and was enthralled by what Li had to say. "I had heard a lot of so-called qigong masters speak over the previous years," he told us. "Most of them were fakes, or had a very low level of cultivation. The minute Master Li began to speak, I knew that we were in the presence of a remarkable person."

Ye is no ordinary judge of character. In 1999, he was the deputy director of the computer division of the Public Security Bureau. Ye is now in his sixties, and seemingly frail, but the history of the Chinese Communist Party is in his bones. He joined it at the age of nineteen, while an engineering student at Beijing's most prestigious university, and remained a true believer for many years — at least for as long as the Party allowed its policies to be questioned. "Then," he said, "we awoke one morning to find that everyone who had been openly critical had been arrested, taken away without a trace, and branded as counter-revolutionaries. They were my senior classmen, mentors, people I had looked up to."

Overnight, Ye was called upon to denounce the activities of those whom he'd most revered. Dismayed, he began to play a sort of double game. Publicly, he survived, continuing with his duties. Secretly, since "it was impossible to talk with anyone to discuss what was happening," he began to analyze every Party policy and position, as well as their deleterious impact on the country.

One can only guess at the tradeoffs he was forced to make in order to ensure his own safety, and that of his family. By the late 1980s, he and his wife were exhausted both physically and mentally after years of overwork, living at near-starvation levels. "There was never enough food," he told us, "even though I was being paid at one of the higher wage levels allowed." The Cultural Revolution had left all the Party's senior members debilitated in mind and body: "We would go to the hospital and be told by the doctors that there was nothing they could do for us." In desperation, Ye turned to traditional medicines. It was in this last-ditch frame of mind that he attended Li's debut in Beijing.

Ye almost immediately became one of Li's original disciples. Having embraced Falun Dafa, his health improved. While still at his post in the Security Bureau, he helped to organize both the Falun Gong Research Society and the first tentative network of teaching centres. Those were the heady days when a sort of dual citizenship was still possible. The Research Society was officially sanctioned by the government for many years, and Ye remembers that "when we held our seminars, more than half of those who attended were Party members."

Those days would come to an abrupt end in 1999, when — for one reason or another — Li miscalculated, playing right into the hands of President Jiang Zemin. (Ye, by the way, suggests that Jiang is, in truth, isolated and disliked by the inner power circles of the Politburo, does not deserve to lead the country, and has already embarked on the fatal steps that will lead inevitably to his own downfall and that of the Communist Party. All this may comfort Ye, but it sounds like whistling in the dark, considering that Jiang is sitting in the President's office, and Ye is in hiding.) It now appears that the post–Zhongnanhai protest "lull" was orchestrated by Jiang, who used the period of negotiation between the Party and Falun Gong to find out which side everyone was on, the better to flush out Falun Gong sympathizers within his regime. Then, on July 20, 1999, he pounced.

The Persecution of the Falun Gong

*H*ere we should make it plain that the chronology of events that follows stems from many sources. First and foremost are sworn depositions made by Falun Gong members. Their claims have been largely substantiated by various human rights groups, including Amnesty International, and by the investigations of foreign journalists. Other facts and figures come from the Centre for Human Rights and Democracy in China, and from Falun Gong's Web site postings.

Finally, we have been able to elicit statements directly from Falun Gong disciples currently resident in North America. Many of these versions of events would be vigorously disputed by the Chinese government, but we believe that the vast majority are true in every particular. Although they will take the most skeptical and jaded reader aback, there are two points to bear in mind. First, our listing is by no means complete; we have been highly selective in our examples. And, in fact, a complete reckoning would be impossible to arrive at. No one really knows how many people have died, especially in out-of-the-way regions. The second point offers scant consolation and must remain to a large degree a matter of speculation: If it hadn't been for the support of Party members, who despite their divided loyalties managed to urge or exercise a modicum of restraint, things could have been far worse.

On the night of July 20, some seventy people considered to be the "inner circle" of Falun Gong were arrested in raids in and around Beijing. One was Li Chang, who had been instrumental in organizing the demonstration at the Zhongnanhai. He was also the head of the Public Security Bureau's computer department. With the core group under lock and key, the authorities began to make political examples of lesser members.

That same day, Dong Buyun, age thirty-six, an elementary schoolteacher from Linyi, in Shandong Province, was arrested and jailed in Beijing, where she'd gone to demonstrate outside the Zhongnanhai. Weeks later, she would be escorted back to her home town by the police, put under guard, and watched day and night. The local police demanded that she recant her membership in Falun Gong. She refused, saying that she'd rather give up her job. The next morning, she was dead, having conveniently committed suicide by jumping out a bathroom window. The police cremated her body without first notifying her family.

Throughout the country, China's public security authorities confiscated Falun Gong literature, as well as portraits and busts of Li Hongzhi, from practitioners' homes. During the first week of the crackdown, an estimated 30,000 practitioners were detained. A third of that number were arrested in central Beijing, where swarms of police were detailed to stand guard on roads, particularly the Avenue of Eternal Peace, which led to the Zhongnanhai. Hundreds of uniformed and plain-clothes officers lined both sides of these access routes, while riot police waited on standby in trucks. No vehicle without a special permit could approach the compound, which immediately took on the appearance of an armed camp.

Elsewhere, police beat many of the 2,000 Falun Gong members who marched on government offices in Liaoning Province to protest the detention of seven leaders arrested there. About 100 members gathered outside the Xinhua news agency offices in the Happy Valley region of Hong Kong and submitted a letter demanding the release of their imprisoned fellow practitioners. Predictably, Kan Hung-cheung, who'd organized the petition, was himself arrested.

On July 22, more than 25,000 Falun Gong members besieged government offices in at least ten of China's major cities. In Beijing, police rounded up the demonstrators, most of whom were elderly men and middle-aged women, and took them in buses to stadiums located on the outskirts of the city, a useful tactic dating back to events in Argentina and Chile during the 1970s. Officials at the stadiums were reported as saying that "lots and lots" more protesters were detained in gymnasium complexes, but refused to estimate the number.

One protester, Fung Lin, a fifty-two-year-old schoolteacher, explained that she would continue her sit-down vigil "until my night shift. Then my husband will take my place, and I will come back after work or tomorrow morning."

Xing Shufang, a worker at the Dagang Oil Field in Tianjin, was one of those arrested and taken to a stadium. "We came to Beijing to appeal, and were arrested the next day," she said. "We were detained in the Fengtai Stadium. There were tens of thousands of practitioners there. The police beat us, made us stand in the burning sun, and did not provide us with water or food. Finally we were transferred back to our local police stations, and detained under the accusation of 'disturbing social order.'"

Released a month later, Xing at once returned to Beijing to demonstrate again. At this time, she was detained at the Tiananmen Police Station for twenty-four hours. "There, I saw a practitioner from Handan beaten up," she said. "His face was bruised. He was ordered to bark like a dog and was denied access to water and toilets. The station became so crowded that it could not hold any more practitioners, so we were transferred to the Changping Detention Center. Some practitioners were robbed and taken outside and beaten by policemen. They were wounded all over their bodies. We had no choice but to start a hunger strike. We encouraged each other by reciting Teacher Li's articles. The police heard us and beat us up again. They also made us stand in the sun. Many practitioners collapsed. Some lost consciousness. Finally I was transferred back to the Tianjin Dagang Oil Field police station."

Back in Hong Kong, Falun Gong members presented a letter headlined "Where is Truth?" to local government officials. It stated that "Falun teachings instruct us on how to develop truth, compassion, and tolerance. Is it criminal to learn how to be a good person?" In addition, Falun Gong Web sites worldwide began to post appeals to members, asking that they "protect the people" by demanding the release of imprisoned practitioners. Members in China were exhorted to explain Falun Gong's aims to local or regional government representatives. Li Hongzhi, for his part, maintained a resolute silence.

The government, of course, had no wish to hear anyone's views on Falun Gong's hopes and aspirations. In mid-July, the Politburo held a closed session, in the course of which a senior member made a speech (later leaked to the Hong Kong media) asserting that Falun Gong posed a "frontal threat" to the Party's hold on power. Should the disorder caused by the practitioners spread, he said, the government would have no choice but to declare the practice of Falun Gong illegal. This suggestion went well beyond previous directives instructing both local police forces and the PAP to remain on alert in preparation for mass arrests of members who continued to demonstrate. This speech was the first intimation of the draconian legislation to come.

Nonetheless, demonstrations continued unabated around the country. Some 10,000 practitioners mounted a protest at the government headquarters in Guangzhou. In Shenzhen, another eight hundred staged a sit-in designed, in the words of Zhang Xiaohua, to "explain to government officials who we are and what we are doing." Zhang had taken the day off from her factory job in order to attend. She and her companions were loaded onto a bus, taken to Hongling Secondary School, and locked in its sports stadium under tight security.

In downtown Shanghai, hundreds of Falun Gong members staged a sit-in at People's Square with less dire results than usual:

Witnesses reported that they left voluntarily without incident. In Hong Kong, followers threatened to protest outside Xinhua's offices for as long as fellow practitioners were detained on the mainland. The next day, after Falun Gong's Web sites had posted news of the latest arrests, some one hundred practitioners returned to mount another demonstration. "We are completely non-political, but the mainland government feels threatened by the sheer number of our followers," said one.

Obviously so. On July 23, the government made good its threat by announcing emergency legislation that banned Falun Gong. A state television broadcast declared it to be an illegal organization that had "seduced the masses with a mixture of religion, superstition, and traditional breathing exercises." This was followed by an order from the Ministry of Civil Affairs, which banned all public Falun Gong activities, including dissemination of materials in any form. The penalty was imprisonment, and the order was retroactive. A high-ranking government official shrugged off the prospect of further protests in response to these edicts. "We will be able to cope with any amount of reaction," he said.

The next day, in San Francisco, between two and three hundred American practitioners gathered at the Chinese consulate, and presented staff members with a letter from Li Hongzhi, entitled "A Brief Statement of Mine." It called for "all governments, international organizations, and people of good will worldwide to extend their support and assistance to us in order to resolve the present crisis." Li also expressed concern for his mother and sisters, who at the time remained in China. "It is said that the police intend to detain them," he wrote.

Simultaneously, officials of the People's Liberation Army declared that their forces should "take the lead in eliminating the influence" of Falun Gong, so as to "encourage healthy trends and scientific thought, and to maintain social stability."

Xinhua, the state news agency, did its part by stepping up anti–Falun Gong propaganda, noting that the group was guilty of "engaging in illegal activities, advocating superstition, spreading fallacies, hoodwinking people, inciting and creating disturbances, and jeopardizing social stability." Li came in for special censure, denounced as a fraud who'd driven ordinary Chinese into "confusion, fear, loss of reason, stupor, and hysteria." Indeed, he was accused of everything short of infanticide and poisoning wells. According to Xinhua, Li was personally responsible for between 700 and 1,400 (the numbers varied) deaths, because he had convinced followers to stop taking prescribed medications. No real evidence to back up this claim was produced.

Not to be outdone, President Jiang weighed in, straining the bounds of credulity by comparing Falun Gong with the Japanese Aum cult, which (as mentioned earlier) had released poison gas aboard the Tokyo subway, killing scores of innocent people. Also floated around at this time was what may or may not be a Chinese urban myth — the almost inevitable charge that at least one man had slit open his stomach in search of the metaphorical falun.

Li responded with a statement charging that the Chinese authorities had attempted to brainwash his followers during their detention, forcing them to watch "fabricated" videotapes that included, among other things, the alleged directive to stop taking medicine. He also reiterated that he could not prevent practitioners from demonstrating if they wished. "I did not ask them to go out onto the streets," he said. "I don't have any control over them."

Nonetheless, at this time, he granted an interview to Radio France International, stating that "if the problem can be resolved without violence, through dialogue, if I have done something wrong, I would agree to go to China to explain matters to the government." He added that he was "disposed to adjust and to adapt Falun Gong a little, according to the government's requirements. But I still do not understand why it has fought Falun Gong with such violence." He speculated that the government's measures may have been spurred by the fact that "there are a lot of people involved, in particular many members of the Communist Party. That is what is shaking the government. As for me, I am just a simple person working free for the good of the people."

Or perhaps not. At about this time, the government began to release a barrage of more prosaic accusations. If Li could not be tarred as the leader of an "evil cult," he might at least be guilty of money grubbing. If this idea could be planted, it would weaken someone who billed himself as the "supreme Buddha," aloof from and devoid of worldly ambition.

The authorities, either through reports published by Xinhua or broadcast on state-run radio and television stations, claimed that Li had accumulated large sums of money by holding training classes. In 1993 and 1994, he was alleged to have made almost 430,000 yuan (over $50,000 U.S.) in the city of Changchun alone by teaching and selling books, plus an additional 789,000 yuan elsewhere, for a grand total of almost $150,000 U.S.

Every little bit added up. For instance, Li supposedly held classes in Harbin over the course of several days, which, at 53 yuan per ticket, gained him $24,000 U.S. All this, if true, was of course entirely legal; Li didn't compel people to attend his lectures or buy Falun Gong materials. With the proceeds, however, he was alleged to have bought expensive automobiles and luxury houses in both Beijing and Changchun, which he held in the names of his relatives. He was also alleged to have evaded paying taxes for a number of years.

Li chose not to respond to these allegations, nor did he offer his supporters much in the way of moral support during their hours of travail. Never once did Li clearly and unequivocally tell his long-suffering practitioners to stop demonstrating. From New York, he reminded them of what he'd written: "It is wrong to think that you are bound to attain the perfection if I am with you, and that you will not if I am not with you. Take the Buddhists for example: Sakyamuni [the Buddha] passed away more than two thousand years ago. Haven't they carried forward his teachings and practised them wholeheartedly? Therefore, it's up to you whether you practise or not."

Back in Beijing, police spokesmen added a novel twist to the mix, assuring practitioners that they wouldn't be charged under the new legislation if they voluntarily came forward and denounced Falun Gong. But, they warned, those who protested and organized had clear "ulterior political motives" and would be dealt with accordingly.

About this time, it was also alleged that the practitioners were a dwindling band, who would sooner or later exhaust their capacity to protest. Far from the up to 100 million followers the government had previously claimed existed, the latest story suggested that the actual number of Falun Gong adherents was a paltry 2 million, based on a recent survey conducted by the Public Security Bureau. If so, they surely posed no clear and present danger to the state, especially since many were under some form of detention. But by this time, any old accusation was being flung around without regard for its logical consequence.

At the end of July 1999, despite the official ban, small numbers of practitioners continued to descend on the Zhongnanhai compound almost daily. Intercepted by police at the checkpoints, they were promptly hustled onto buses and whisked away to uncertain fates. Followers also defied the legislation by gathering elsewhere throughout Beijing. In Yuetan (the Altar of the Moon Park), they could be seen exercising to the accompaniment of a tape-recorded voice that chanted instructions while soft music played. Their leader, a man in his mid-thirties, had seen the tele-vision proclamation banning Falun Gong, but said: "If you believe something is good, just go on." Another practitioner added that many of his fellow believers were in the park as well, but were too afraid to do any more than watch from a safe distance. "We are not free," he said. "What is really free is our minds. There, we can think everything we want to think."

By this time, protesters around the world were stepping up their activities, gathering at Chinese consulates — notably in Toronto and in Australia — where they were repelled by means of high-pressure water hoses. But ordinary practitioners in Western countries also reported that Chinese agents had begun campaigns of threatening phone calls and visits similar to the one described in our prologue, during which Falun Gong groups were accosted in parks and other public places.

By August 1999, it was unclear whether the government's intimidation tactics, coupled with the legislative ban, would suc-ceed in dampening the enthusiasm of Falun Gong practitioners. Many, as we've already mentioned, were middle-aged and elderly people who'd initially become involved with the movement only in hopes that it would improve their health. Perhaps a finite number would be willing to risk life and limb by evidencing their support.

But throughout August, the police were forced to seal off large portions of Tiananmen Square in response to renewed early-morning sit-ins conducted by hundreds of practitioners, who were immediately detained and taken to suburban stadiums. It was becoming apparent that the government, by means of its heavy-handed repression, had succeeded only in strengthening the practitioners' resolve, turning what might otherwise have been dismissed as a nuisance into the nation's largest — indeed, its only — opposition group.

The crackdown had added credibility, and bolstered the practitioners' unflagging will to carry on. When released from temporary detention in the sports stadiums, they would respond by returning to the protest lines as soon as they could. The authorities tried to thin out their ranks with the promise that if ordinary members (as opposed to leaders) made a clean break from the group, they'd face no further consequences. But all to no avail — the protesters just kept on coming.

Meanwhile, the incessant denunciation of Li Hongzhi continued. At its height, China's national television evening newscast was extended from thirty minutes to two hours nightly. At times, more than three-quarters of the items aired were attacks on Falun Gong in general and on Li in particular.

On July 30, the government had issued an order for Li's arrest, and called for international help in apprehending and detaining him. Xinhua, the state news agency, added that cooperation had been sought from Interpol member states, but did not specify whether Beijing would request his extradition. The litany of charges against him was familiar: "superstition and witchery, malicious fallacies, and instigating chaos to destroy social stability." The arrest order accused him of plotting to organize gatherings, demonstrations, and other activities without applying for permits according to law, thus committing the heinous crime of disturbing public order.

Li's photograph and Chinese and American travel documents were widely circulated, in hopes that all public security departments and border checkpoints would spring to attention and track him down. From New York, Falun Gong spokespersons said the warrant was "based upon fabricated evidence," and called upon the U.S. government to protect Li, which it showed every sign of doing. In Washington, D.C., Li's aides said that he was safe as long as he stayed put. "We spoke to the State Department this morning," said one, "and they told us there was no problem."

Not content with these measures, the government propaganda machine then corralled an eighty-one-year-old war hero named Li Qihua, who obligingly denounced Falun Gong. Li Qihua (not to be confused with General Li Zang, who acted as an intermediary at the time of the Zhongnanhai demonstration) had joined the revolution when he was nine, and had taken part in the Long March. As a lieutenant-general in the People's Liberation Army, he was also the highest-ranking Communist Party member to have publicly declared his membership in Falun Gong.

Now, he was quick to state that he knew nothing of Falun Gong before 1993, when his wife fell ill. "On the advice of other people, I started to try Falun Gong with her," he explained. "Because of my high position, people encouraged and helped me to write an article which mistakenly promoted Falun Gong."

In fact, like Li Zang, General Li Qihua was a prominent leader within the Falun Gong movement, and had also worked behind the scenes in hopes of brokering an accommodation with the government. His excellent connections made him a perfect ambassador. Why he chose to write the article in question remains in doubt, but he did in fact write it. Unfortunately for him, it appeared shortly before the initial protest at the Zhongnanhai. He then received a visit from the Central Military Commission, whose attentions moved him to express "anger and shock" at the practitioners' actions. He further stated that he had "made a study of the important speech of Jiang Zemin, and was educated," adding that he felt deeply "betrayed" by his former fellows, particularly those who'd suggested that he pen the article. In all, this sorry sequence of events followed a time-worn script: the heavy-handed confrontation, the abject confession, a surrender to thought-reform techniques, and a now-I-see-the-light denunciation.

During the first week in August, Li Hongzhi made more frequent use of his Web site, asking the international community to pressure the Chinese authorities into ceasing their "brutal actions," which he compared to the dark days of the Cultural Revolution. But, he added, the oppressors "cannot change the will and the heart of the people. If they crack down on Falun Gong, the people would lose trust in the state and the leadership."

He also spoke out in the form of an interview published in the August 8, 1999, issue of the *New York Times Magazine*. In it, Li disavowed any comparison with Gandhi, and claimed not to view political action as an agent of change in people's lives. "I want to teach people to be good and not be involved in politics," he said. "I myself never want to get involved in politics. I don't care for it. Governments focus only on the problem at hand, instead of looking at what has caused this problem in the first place. If ordinary people's society does not become more virtuous, any number of problems may occur, and I cannot concern myself with this prospect. I am only responsible to the practitioners of Falun Gong." Li's interview took place in person on July 22; this was the last time any neutral party laid eyes on him.

Unimpressed by Li's remarks, the Chinese authorities stepped up their propaganda assault, launching a nation-wide campaign to seize and burn Li's books. Xinhua reported that public security forces had destroyed 130,000 books and 27,000 audio and videotapes in the central city of Wuhan alone. More than 1 million books were said to have been confiscated and presumably consigned to the flames. Books and other publications were also cut off at the pass — notably in Dandong City, where the police arrested six workers and a supervisor at a printing plant. They were charged with producing outlawed material.

The government did not overlook the new technologies. In late July, it started shutting down Falun Gong Web sites and arresting their operators. At about this time, a curious war of words began taking place in cyberspace, as e-mail became the only way for overseas practitioners to contact their counterparts on the mainland. But the police were computer literate, too. Soon, Hong Kong practitioners began to post warnings on the movement's sites, claiming that several anonymous e-mails had been sent from U.S. sources to mainland followers, urging them to "stand up to protect" their fellow believers. The Hong Kong group cautioned that these messages were bogus, and had been concocted by agents of the Chinese intelligence service, in hopes that mainland practitioners would be roused to engage in even more avid demonstrations. "Master Li has reiterated that we should act according to law," the Hong Kong group advised. "We would never encourage anyone to act against the government, because our creed is forbearance. We suspect that these e-mails were sent by people who hate us. They want to fan the flames and force the government to take more drastic action against us. Our overseas members have already posted a clarification on our Web sites, but we are afraid the mainland practitioners cannot connect with them because of the government's electronic blockade." This clarification ended with a request that followers remain calm, and believe only those messages sent directly by Li himself.

Nor did the government ignore other enemies of the state. In early August, a court sentenced Liu Xianbin, one of the organizers of the 1989 Tiananmen Square protest and a leading member of the Chinese Democratic Party, to thirteen years in prison for subversion. This equalled the sentence already meted out to Xu Wenli, the CDP's leader, but exceeded the terms imposed on three other members, who received twelve, nine, and eight years behind bars.

Throughout August 1999, Falun Gong practitioners — especially those in Hong Kong, who, because of the island's less repressive rule, appeared to enjoy more freedom of expression than mainland Chinese — continued to call for international assistance. On August 2, about two hundred protesters gathered outside Xinhua's Hong Kong offices, standing silently with eyes closed and performing meditation exercises.

But the police did not intervene, even when some of the demonstrators approached the building's locked gates and left a letter addressed to President Jiang. It requested that the ban against Falun Gong be rescinded, complained that Beijing had spread lies and half-truths about the group's practices, and asked that the Chinese government establish a dialogue with Li Hongzhi. "We hope you understand that Falun Gong members have nothing to do with politics," it said. "We only want to be good people." As well, the letter urged intervention on the part of the United Nations and the Red Cross, and concluded by announcing plans to screen Falun Gong videos in public places for people who could no longer get information from the usual sources, since many Hong Kong bookshops had stopped stocking Li's writings.

President Jiang did not take kindly to these appeals; he was at the time primarily concerned with lobbying the U.S. Congress to grant China permanent "most favoured nation" trading status, as a prelude to its hoped-for acceptance as a member of the World Trade Organization (WTO). Similar meetings were underway with members of the European Community.

These encounters all tended to unfold in much the same way. Western delegates would begin by bemoaning the latest evidence of flagrant human rights violations, and would ask the Chinese what they proposed to do about them. China's responses were both public and scathing. It denounced flagrant American interference in and subversion of China's domestic affairs, dismissed the human-rights-abuse allegations as fantasies, and accused the West of attempting to use the allegations in an effort to gain the upper hand in the WTO negotiations.

Next, rather than moving towards a dialogue with Falun Gong in Hong Kong or anywhere else, Jiang asked the Thai government (and, once again, Interpol) to arrest Li if he attempted to visit his estimated 1,000 followers in Bangkok, where they were planning to hold a conference. (They did hold it, but Li didn't show up.) Failing that, Jiang hoped that Li might be taken into custody in London, where Falun Gong's first British conference was slated for August 29. (It also unfolded without Li's participation.)

Interpol replied to the latter request by pointing out that Li couldn't be detained in Britain because Falun Gong hadn't been declared illegal there. (Interpol tends to tread very carefully when it comes to politically sensitive cases. For extradition to take place, an offense must be recognized by both countries involved.) The U.S., for its part, refused the Chinese government's demand.

Back in mainland China, the tribulations of the practitioners continued. Ying Chen, eighteen, a student from Jiamusi, was being transferred back home after her arrest in Beijing, where she had been beaten while in police custody. She did not reach her destination alive. It remains unclear whether she died jumping from the train in an attempt to escape, whether she intended to commit suicide rather than endure further torture, or whether she was thrown from the train.

By September, the purge of Falun Gong practitioners had

spread to the hinterland. In the small town of Linglong in Shandong Province, more than fifty adherents were arrested and taken to a detention centre. One group of fifteen was allowed, in total, less than a cup of water a day. Sometimes none was provided at all.

The detainees were regularly insulted and beaten. Five or six police officers took turns subjecting Lu Caimei to electric shocks. This continued for over two hours, until she finally lost consciousness. The chief of police and two of his officers tied Chang Dongfang down and beat her for more than eight hours over two successive nights. Her face was swollen and she had internal bleeding. She was also tortured with electric shocks. On September 22, Li Wende was suspended by his wrists and beaten throughout the night. Li Jinguo was beaten until he could not stand. Wei Qihua and Wei Jinqin, both nearly sixty years old, were forced to stand for hours with their arms outstretched and legs bent.

All of these practitioners were detained for more than forty days. At last, they were released after their relatives signed, and left their fingerprints on, "pledges" binding the practitioners to abandon Falun Gong. Another condition of their release was that they, or their relatives, had to pay between 2,000 and 6,000 yuan (the higher figure represents about half the annual income of an average Chinese worker) to the police department.

Late in September, another practitioner, Zhao Dong, thirty-eight, who came from Jixi in Heilongjiang, jumped or was thrown from a train while under police guard. He too had been arrested in Beijing, and was being returned to local custody. In Anshan, in Liaoning Province, three practitioners named Wang Wei, Hu Shuzhi, and Ning Guiying were arrested in their homes, taken to the local detention centre, hung from a heating pipe, and beaten all night long.

These scenes were repeated in hundreds of localities. In

Zhangxing Town, five female practitioners were taken to the local police station, ordered to squat on the ground, and told to read books denouncing Falun Gong. When they refused, they were beaten on their faces and heads throughout the afternoon. Eventually, one of them was transferred to the detention centre in Zhaoyuan. The rest were not allowed to sleep. If they did, they were beaten. They attempted to practise a meditation exercise, but were observed by a guard, who summoned a police official. He arrived, and ordered that the practitioners be beaten with rubber clubs. One of them, Zhao Jinhua, age forty-two, was also subjected to electric shocks administered by means of an old-fashioned telephone. The police asked her if she would abandon Falun Gong, but she refused, so they continued to crank the handle of the telephone, causing her to lose consciousness three times.

Then the four practitioners were forced to stand barefoot on the concrete floor. Zhao Jinhua leaned against the wall. Her face was waxen. She fell down with her eyes closed, and was transferred to a Zhangxing hospital. There she was given drugs before being sent back to the police station. She felt pressure in her chest, there was blood in her urine, and she was unable to eat.

The practitioners were detained for almost a week, during which time Zhao's condition worsened. A police officer remarked that she had gotten what she deserved. At last, she fell and could not get up again. She was returned to the hospital, and died while doctors were administering an electrocardiogram. An autopsy revealed that she had suffered multiple wounds and subcutaneous bleeding, the results of repeated beatings with blunt objects.

At least her death came reasonably quickly, unlike the death of Zhu Shaolan, age fifty, of Jinzhou, who was arrested along with other local practitioners for collecting signatures for a letter that appealed for their freedom to practise Falun Gong. She died on October 5, following a lengthy hunger strike.

That same day, Lu Chunna arrived back home in Daqinjia Town, having been arrested in Beijing. Local police officers surrounded her and beat her. When she lost consciousness, they thought she was pretending to be dead, and continued the beating. They then attempted to revive her with cold water, and when this failed, transferred her to the local hospital. When her relatives arrived, the police told them that her condition was caused by her refusal to eat anything for three days. Released from hospital, she was jailed again for two weeks, then sent home again. Later the police went to her home, demanded that she pay a fee for being transported there, and threatened to confiscate the salaries of her elder sister and father.

Wang Guoping, age forty, also travelled to Beijing to take part in the protests. He was arrested, stripped of his clothes, and soaked with cold water. In mid-October he was transferred to the liaison office of the Jilin provincial government in Beijing. Two days later he, too, conveniently "committed suicide" by jumping from an eighth-floor window.

On October 9, Lee Yuk-suet, fifty-one, a resident of Hong Kong, was forced to barricade herself inside an apartment in the mainland city of Shenzhen, where she had gone on a business trip to sell cosmetics. The police outside demanded that she surrender to them because they had discovered not only that she practised Falun Gong at home, but that she had been approached by followers in Shenzhen to sign a petition protesting the death of Zhao Jinhua, described above. "They had no warrant or search order," she said. "They refused to tell me why they wanted me to go with them. I said I had the right to know why, and they replied, 'You don't have any rights, you only have the duty to obey.'" Fortunately, Ms. Lee was saved by several newspaper reporters, whose timely arrival caused the police to retreat.

On October 22, when President Jiang went to London, he ran into a rough reception. He was forced to enter 10 Downing Street via the back door, because Falun Gong practitioners and other protesters (including members of the Free Tibet Campaign) had assembled up and down Whitehall. Nonetheless, Jiang enjoyed lunch with the British Prime Minister Tony Blair, and with the Australian press baron Rupert Murdoch, who has numerous business interests in China. After their meal, Jiang and Murdoch reconvened at the British Museum, where Jiang opened an exhibit (co-sponsored by Murdoch) of ancient Chinese treasures.

On October 25, 1999, the Ministry of Public Security upped the ante by charging Li Hongzhi, the Falun Dafa Research Society, and several individual Falun Gong practitioners with espionage, for having allegedly illegally obtained fifty-nine state documents, ranging from confidential to top-secret, some of which were then passed by unspecified means to foreign countries. This novel charge was accompanied by yet another round of more familiar statements, accusing Falun Gong practitioners of "besieging" various government venues.

All contact with Falun Gong had, of course, been outlawed since July, when the movement was banned. But on October 28, members of Beijing's foreign press corps defied the ban by agreeing to attend a secret meeting hosted by underground practitioners. Journalists were contacted via e-mail, then smuggled to a suburban Buddhist temple after a complicated taxi ride across the capital. (Later, when the location was identified, the authorities would question the journalists who'd taken part, and temporarily confiscate their press credentials and residence permits.)

During this meeting, reporters were given detailed information about the government's ongoing suppression, including the latest incident. Earlier that day, a dozen practitioners had been seized as they were about to enter the giant red Gate of Heavenly Peace, the entrance to the former Imperial Palace, also known as the Forbidden City. They had attempted to mingle with a crowd of tourists, but were identified by plainclothes security agents. Its siren blaring, a police van raced from the palace grounds, across a white marble bridge once reserved for the emperor and empress. The practitioners were herded into it and whisked away. One man resisted, but was forced aboard after a brief struggle. A Western journalist who photographed the arrests was collared by police, who confiscated his camera and destroyed the film.

On October 31, the National People's Congress Standing Committee voted unanimously in favour of severe punishments for anyone involved in "promoting cult activities." The new law set a penalty of three to seven years in prison for "those who set up or use superstitious sects and secret societies or superstition to deceive people and cause the death of others," as well as those who demonstrated, disrupted social order, or printed or distributed material that spread "malicious fallacies." The law set even stiffer penalties for those who worked with foreigners or residents of other provinces. As well, the Security Bureau stated that trials were expected to begin soon against some of the thousands of Falun Gong members who still languished in detention.

Not surprisingly, Falun Gong practitioners responded with a fresh round of demonstrations, appearing in Tiananmen Square for six straight days. Thirty were arrested in the first few hours of the first day. The police were prepared; hundreds stood ready and waiting. Some practitioners walked calmly to the buses, while others cried. A Communist Party official estimated that more than 3,000 people had been taken away by the time these protests ended, but they were a fraction of the total numbers involved. Thousands of Falun Gong practitioners arrived daily from other parts of the country, and once again attempted to make life difficult for the police by refusing to reveal where they lived, so that they could not be sent back to detention centres in their own area. To counter the fresh influx, police warned Beijing

landlords and homeowners not to rent rooms to the practitioners. Those who did were subject to heavy fines.

On November 1, North American newspapers revealed that
Li Hongzhi's wife, Li Rui, had been given a 4,600-square-foot
house located in Princeton, New Jersey. The gift had in fact
taken place much earlier in the year — to be precise, just three
weeks after the Zhongnanhai demonstration and Li's mysterious
in-and-out-the-windows junket to Beijing. It had been purchased
in Mrs. Li's name by John Sun, a wealthy lampshade manufac-
turer and a Falun Gong enthusiast. Sun confirmed that he had
paid $580,000 U.S. for the house, in gratitude for "the great
health benefit that I have obtained through practising Falun
Gong." He added that he had bought the house while Li was
travelling, and that he (Sun) had had Mrs. Li sign the paperwork
without telling her what it entailed. Li's spokesmen maintained
that he had refused the gift, and Sun said that, given Li's refusal,
he would occupy the property himself, even though he owned
another home on Staten Island that served as the registered
address for the Eastern U.S. Buddha's Study (Falun Dafa)
Association, a non-profit organization.

On November 2, when 217 more practitioners were arrested
in Beijing alone, and twelve female schoolteachers in Jilin
Province were sentenced without trial to one-year terms in
labour camps for meditating in public places, a bizarre sidebar
sprang to light. State news agencies reported that police had
smashed a "copycat sect" known as Guo (or National) Gong,
which claimed supernatural powers of its own, and took care to
offer its own synthesis of Buddhism, Taoism, Confucianism,
martial arts, and traditional medicine. Its leader Liu Jineng and
two of his senior disciples were arrested for numerous crimes,
including "illegal management." According to the *Sichuan Daily*,
Liu preached "a bright future" illuminated by his alleged ability
to "open up secret powers" and "reveal the mysteries of magic."

Also routed was a group called Cibei (or Compassion) Gong, whose founder Xiao Yun had apparently made a good living from sales of books and cassette tapes. But Xiao had a dark side: reports alleged that he had raped at least four of his followers, claiming that enlightenment came through having sex with him.

Despite these distractions, President Jiang's primary target remained Falun Gong, and there was absolutely no doubt in anyone's mind that he personally directed its repression. On November 5, at his order, the practitioners who had organized the clandestine press conference of October 28 were tracked down and arrested. Jiang had been particularly outraged by this act of defiance, and more than 1,000 police had been dispatched to find the site where it took place. They did so by analyzing pictures released by the Western media that offered clues to the site's location.

Jiang also decreed that anti–Falun Gong measures were to be stepped up all around the country, under the banner of the Three Emphases, a separate campaign that stressed the importance of the correct political line, of righteousness, and of learning from the Marxist canon. Party members in factories and universities were given fresh and highly detailed instruction on rooting out the pernicious influence of Falun Gong on fellow workers and students.

On November 9, two middle-aged women from Weifang named Zhang Yuhua and Wang Lianfang decided to travel to Beijing to make appeals on behalf of Falun Gong. They were intercepted by police at the local train station, and handed over to a group of government officials, who beat them severely and stole their money. That night, other members of the town government beat them with rubber clubs. Later they were transferred to the Zhaoyuan City police department, which held them for fifteen days. Their relatives visited them, and took photographs of the bruises on their bodies.

On November 10, Fu Caixia, a practitioner from Daqinjia Town, managed to travel to Beijing, where she handed in a letter at the entrance of the Appealing Office. Several officers accosted her, seized her letter, and took her to a hotel, where they beat her unconscious. They then handcuffed her and locked her in a closet. Transferred back home, she suffered further beatings at the hands of other officers, who demanded a payment of 10,000 yuan and threatened to take away her farming tractor. One officer wrote out a draft mortgage document, then forced her to copy it and mark it with her thumbprint. After doing so, she was transferred to a local police station for criminal detention.

On November 16, during a visit to Beijing by the United Nations' Secretary General Kofi Annan, who issued a typically anemic plea for restraint on the Chinese government's part, more than a dozen Falun Gong practitioners unfurled a Falun Gong banner in Tiananmen Square, and were immediately hauled away.

From November 1999 to February 2000, the American government moved swiftly on Falun Gong. Its motives may in retrospect be suspect, but its actions were unprecedented, surprising onlookers who recalled that the U.S. has consistently backed all manner of dictators worldwide whose body count far exceeds President Jiang's, and for whom torture was, and in many cases remains, an instrument of state policy.

On November 18, a Joint Congressional Resolution roundly condemned China's actions — a remarkably rapid and pointed response to the woes of a third-world spiritual group. Certainly there had been very little in the way of such official condemnation of religious persecution in India, Indonesia, Europe, Japan, Saudi Arabia, or Latin America, especially when the regime in question happened to be a U.S. ally, or when U.S. economic interests were at stake.

On November 24, four foreign Falun Gong practitioners were detained in the course of a demonstration mounted by residents of Guangzhou, but were released a few days later, only to be expelled from the country. The Chinese citizens arrested with them remained in custody. On November 30, the Chinese Vice Premier Li Lanqing reportedly stated in a speech to Party members that more than 35,000 practitioners had been detained between July 22 and October 30. The government later clarified his remarks by pointing out that this figure represented the total number of "confrontations," and that, since many people were recidivists, having had multiple encounters with the police, they shouldn't be counted two or three times.

On December 6 (the day that President Clinton, a fervent supporter of China's entry into the WTO, publicly criticized its actions with respect to Falun Gong), President Jiang, determined to crush the development of anything resembling an alternative press, moved to close down all newspapers that printed fewer than 30,000 copies. These smaller enterprises had given state-run publications unwelcome competition in recent years. Now they were to be merged into one single newspaper, managed directly by a pair of government commissions.

More than six months after the initial crackdown, Falun Gong practitioners persisted in their activities, and the authorities maintained their policy of vicious reprisal. On December 15, seven practitioners in Zhaoyuan City were arrested when they turned up at a local police station to present an appeal. They were forced to squat on their toes with arms outstretched, sometimes holding a wooden pole behind their knees. They were also subjected to electric shocks. Despite these tortures, they went to Beijing a week later, and made it as far as Tiananmen Square. One of them, a female practitioner named Liu Xiang, described what then occurred.

At about ten o'clock in the morning, she and two of her

companions began to practise exercises in the square. Within a few seconds, they were arrested by the police. Upon arrival at the Tiananmen Square police station, their interrogation began. The practitioners refused to reveal where they lived. In the early afternoon, an officer named Zhao arrived, punched Ms. Liu in the head, and kicked one of her companions, who had assumed the lotus position. Zhao then ordered the group to strip to their underwear. Strangely, while he issued these orders, he was holding a copy of *Hong Yin*, a collection of poems written by Li Hongzhi. Even more strangely, Zhao went on to talk about his "understanding," stating that he had read Li's other works also, and did not usually beat Falun Gong practitioners because they were "good people." He added, however, that "your teacher is using police officers to upgrade your moral levels." After this remark, he went to sleep.

The next morning, a larger group of practitioners was brought into the police station. If Ms. Liu and her companions attempted to speak with them, they were beaten with a stick. A woman in her fifties who had been severely beaten began to bleed profusely. Ms. Liu demanded to speak to the station's chief officer, but another practitioner observed that they ought to bear their tribulations calmly. Ms. Liu then used tissues in an attempt to stop the other woman's bleeding. That afternoon, the police ordered "a patient with mental illness and two petty criminals" to beat Ms. Liu. She "smiled" as they beat her.

Later, the practitioners were subjected to a form of torture known as "reverse flying," in which victims are suspended upside down, with the arms wrenched outwards. Later, other practitioners were "backhand cuffed" — an excruciating torture in which one arm is forced back over the shoulder, the other forced up behind the back from the waist, and the hands are bound together. Ms. Liu was treated in this way, and her hands were beaten, as were the hands of her companions. She took care to count the beatings. Each round usually consisted of twenty blows.

The next day, another officer took over the interrogation, demanding to know why Liu Xiang and her friends had come to Beijing. She said it was because Falun Dafa had been "banned and defamed" by the authorities. Asked where she would go if she were released, she replied, "I take everywhere as my home."

This officer had not taken part in the previous beatings, and asked who had administered them. She said that it didn't matter, because she had no hatred towards anybody. The officer told her to go home, but she replied that she would not "until innocence was returned to Falun Dafa. I came here nobly, and I will walk out nobly, too." In the end, this officer secured her release, stating that "your wish has been fulfilled. Your goal has been achieved."

On December 16, the government ordered that any and all "qigong activities" must be "small, scattered, localized and voluntary." Nor would devotees of qigong be permitted to form any new groups within existing organizations. This followed reports of increased harassment of non–Falun Gong enthusiasts, the arrest of two leaders of such groups, and a ban on qigong exercises in public parks or on government property.

On December 18, the former Portuguese island colony of Macau counted the hours until it would be handed over to China, which would then assume control of it as a "special administrative region." The preparations for this transfer of authority included the expulsion of six Falun Gong practitioners, bringing to ten the total number deported. Authorities warned that demonstrators who attempted to disrupt the hand-over ceremonies would face a two-year jail term.

On December 26, four senior members of Falun Gong were sentenced by a Beijing court for obstruction of justice, causing death in the course of cult activities, and illegally obtaining state secrets. Li Chang, of the Zhongnanhai protest, received eighteen years. A former railways official named Wang Zhiwen was sentenced to sixteen years, and two other men, Ji Liewu and Yao Jie, were sent to jail for twelve and seven years respectively.

On January 10, 2000, a U.S.-sponsored resolution before the United Nations Committee on Human Rights (which was scheduled to sit in early March) put Falun Gong's persecution on the agenda, and the European Parliament began to debate a separate resolution that would tie future trade talks to a number of human rights issues.

All this came too late for Gao Xianmin, a forty-one-year-old from Guangzhou. He was arrested in that city's Tianhe Park, where he and ten other practitioners were having lunch, then transferred to the Tangxia Detention Centre. On January 18, his family received notification of his death. The authorities stated that he had lost consciousness after launching a hunger strike. In fact, Gao had been force-fed a high-density mixture of salt and water, while his nose was forcibly covered with wet towels. This is another standard police procedure. Often, as Gao did, the recipient suffocates to death.

On January 21, the Centre for Human Rights and Democracy in China revealed that fifty Falun Gong practitioners had been held for over a month at the Zhoukoudian Psychiatric Hospital, just outside Beijing. Police described them as "repeat offenders," who, having returned to that city on several occasions, were in need of re-education. (The use of psychiatric hospitals as holding tanks for political troublemakers appears to be relatively rare. Only facilities controlled by the Public Security Bureau are involved, because doctors at mainstream hospitals attempt not to participate in these activities.)

On January 24, the Deputy Chief of the People's Liberation Army's general staff began two days of talks in Washington with senior Pentagon officials, the first military contact between the two countries since NATO forces bombed the Chinese embassy in Belgrade, Yugoslavia, killing three and injuring twenty-seven. The U.S. had stated that the bombing was an accident, and in December, had committed $28 million to compensating the embassy for its loss.

On February 3, the U.S. Congress voted in favour of increased military aid to the long-disputed island of Taiwan. The U.S. was, and is, bound by an agreement to come to Taiwan's aid, were it to be attacked by China. A further treaty, which Congress ignored, promised the Chinese that the U.S. would not sell the Taiwanese armaments such as guided missiles and equipment such as enhanced radar for its F-16 jet fighter planes. The Congressional bill was not expected to survive either the Senate or a Presidential veto.

On February 6, 2000, the Chinese welcomed in the Year of the Dragon — traditionally, a period during which caution is thrown to the wind, life has a manic edge, and both successes or disasters tend to come in waves. As a spectacular fireworks display filled the sky above Tiananmen Square, the CNN television network broadcast live coverage of large groups of Falun Gong practitioners being beaten and dragged away. They had converged on the square a few moments before the stroke of midnight, with banners hidden underneath their clothing. These were unfurled and waved at the crowds. In a battle of personality cults, two men attempted to superimpose a portrait of Li Hongzhi on a giant image of Mao Zedong, but were quickly subdued.

Having cleared the square, the police closed it to the public and to tourists. Security officers later refused to confirm how many protesters were arrested during the melee, but unofficial estimates suggest they numbered between 2,000 and 3,000.

The next day, Falun Gong Web sites reported that Jiang Zhaohui, the main organizer of the previous year's clandestine press conference, had been sentenced to jail for twelve years. On February 11, Liu Xuguo, a twenty-nine-year-old factory engineer from Jining, died from injuries to his trachea and lungs brought about by the police forcing a feeding tube down his throat. Liu had begun a hunger strike six days earlier, while being detained at a local "re-education through labour" camp. A nearby hospital did not take the measures necessary to save him.

In mid-February, the U.S. Immigration Department announced that Chinese nationals who sought asylum based on their persecution as Falun Gong practitioners would be granted permission to remain in the United States.

On February 25, the U.S. State Department's *Human Rights Report* devoted a great deal of space to Falun Gong. Over the years, such reports have been in essence subjective instruments of U.S. foreign policy. For example, it's very difficult to find equally scathing denunciations of South American juntas during the 1970s, when military dictators such as Augusto Pinochet seized power in Chile. Thus, many observers saw this year's version as part of the U.S. administration's carrot-and-stick approach, preparatory to a decision on China's entry into the WTO.

The report concluded that every component of China's state security apparatus — that is, the ministries of State Security and Public Security, the Provincial Armed Police, the People's Liberation Army, and the judicial, procuratorial, and penal systems — were jointly responsible for the abuses committed against Falun Gong. The report also noted that the Chinese government's "poor human rights record deteriorated markedly" throughout 1999, as it "continued to suppress dissent, particularly organized dissent . . . the Government continued to commit widespread and well-documented human rights abuses, in violation of internationally accepted norms." This was hardly the sort of behaviour the U.S. wished to be seen as condoning, while it strove to grant China favoured-nation trading status, but that process, the report notwithstanding, had assumed a life of its own.

By the end of February, Jiang's edicts had reduced Falun Gong's practitioners to citizens without status. Reports from many villages and towns in Shandong Province indicated that the police believed it to be open season. In Tangezhuang Township, the local authorities made repeated raids on people's homes, extorting money and confiscating television sets, farm implements, and clothing. Elsewhere, the power supply to practitioners' properties was disconnected. Some followers were detained at their workplaces, and could not return to their families. Others were removed from their posts or dismissed from schools where they were studying.

Many rural areas had been reduced to lawlessness and barbarism. In Heping Village, practitioners suffered tortures such as "being fully fixed." This involves binding a prisoner's head, hands, and feet, then leaving him or her, unable to move, for several days.

At about this time, rumours abounded concerning Li Hongzhi's whereabouts. Stories circulated to the effect that he had left North America and was living secretly in Taiwan, Hong Kong, and other unlikely locales. More dire possibilities arose as well. A Falun Gong Web site posted a photo depicting him sitting cross-legged in meditation, staring out over what appeared to be the Grand Canyon. The accompanying text, which made precious little sense, was interpreted by some as a "goodbye, cruel world" message, and gave rise to speculation that he was dead, perhaps at the hands of assassins. But his steadfast disciples kept repeating what had by now become the party line: "Master Li has not abandoned us. He has always told us that he would only be with us a short time, but the law, the dafa that he has given us, will always be there to guide us."

On March 10, Falun Gong practitioners in Tokyo, Japan, were distressed to learn that the metropolitan government had turned down their application for status as a non-profit organization, on the grounds that Japanese law stipulates that such organizations cannot be "chiefly religious or political." A government source denied that China had anything to do with the decision. "We never imagined that we would be rejected," said a Falun Gong spokesman. "Our group uses religious expressions, but we are not a religion."

On March 15, Chinese Internet users bemoaned what one man described as "the Great Firewall of China," which bars anything except state-approved content and Chinese-registered sites. "As soon as you start downloading something politically forbidden, it comes down and cuts the flow of data," he said. "Your computer just freezes." Sites affected included those operated by the *New York Times*, the *International Herald Tribune*, and, of course, Falun Gong.

On April 25, 2000, a year to the day after the protest at the Zhongnanhai compound, more than a hundred practitioners once again arrived at Tiananmen Square, unfurling banners and meditating. A chaotic scene ensued. Throngs of Chinese tourists ran to witness the arrests, while police loudspeakers ordered the demonstrators to disperse. Many people were accosted in the crowd by plainclothes officers who demanded whether they practised Falun Gong. Foreign tourists, for their part, stood astonished as a group of six women, all carrying children in their arms, were bundled into a van. One protester leaned out a window, raised his fist, and shouted, "The Great Way of Falun is good." The police compelled an American woman to rip the film out of her camera, fearing that she'd photographed this and other events.

On May 13, the Buddha's birthday, thousands of people in many North American and European centres gathered on what had meanwhile been designated World Falun Dafa Day, to pay homage to Li Hongzhi. Unfortunately, they had to be content with bowing to an enormous portrait, since Li declined to put in an appearance anywhere.

Then, on May 18, 2000, the political, economic, and moral landscape that had separated China from the Western world turned upside down. That landscape, mined with accusations of intolerable human rights abuses and darkly clouded by rumours of imminent war over Taiwan, at once became a vast and peaceful frontier, marked only by free trade and high technology. The deal that created and cemented this historic and sweeping reversal of fortune was struck when leaders of the European Economic Community agreed to let the human rights issue drop off the edge of the bargaining table, thus removing a significant barrier to China's eventual acceptance by the WTO.

In return, China agreed to open up the incalculable potential of its financial and telecommunications markets to multinational corporations. A few days later, the U.S. Congress, in celebration of this development, passed legislation that officially granted China permanent favoured-nation status. Capitalism, the Western leaders assured their citizens, would guarantee a bright tomorrow. It might take a while, but a rising tide would lift all political prisoners.

By June 20, 2000, Falun Gong had compiled a lengthy list of atrocities committed by the Chinese police and security forces. In sum, to that date, twenty-four practitioners had died while in police custody, another 50,000 had been imprisoned without trial, and an additional 5,000 were being held in psychiatric hospitals.

Alas, that infamous record is long since out of date. By the end of October 2000 twice as many more would die. This number may only be the tip of the iceberg; more corpses may yet be discovered among the detainees. Indeed, even as you read these words, someone somewhere is writhing in agony, simply because they chose to express their belief in the gospel according to Li Hongzhi.

Three

The Theories and Practices of Li Hongzhi

*I*n this chapter, we shall explore in greater detail the roots of Li Hongzhi's spiritual belief system, and examine whether his teachings square with his more questionable behaviour. In doing so, we have several hurdles to overcome.

The first is Li's ghastly writing style, which he defends on his Web site by arguing that "in order to express the Dafa clearly, I employ them [the rules of grammar and punctuation] as I wish. It is very difficult to use human language to express the high-level, profound principles of the Fa." Perhaps, but it's all we've got to go by.

Li is also on record as stating that he chose not to attend university because he didn't want to end up brain damaged — a defensible decision for a youthful iconoclast. But to assert, as he's done, that he doesn't bother to write grammatically because modern Chinese writers have corrupted their heritage reveals a certain parochialism. Worse, Li's oddball prose turns many of his more interesting ideas into a bewildering spiritual doublespeak

— a far cry from the promise extended by the Falun Gong Web site, which describes his teachings as "profound and extensive, but transmitted in the most simple language."

On the contrary, their transmission will strike many Western readers as bizarre and impenetrable. And, since Li is disinclined to credit his sources, many an hour could be spent debating whether a particular tenet of his system is pulled from Buddhism, Taoism, Confucianism, neo-Confucianism, or out of thin air.

Having followed his myriad twists and turns as far as humanly possible, it's tempting to focus on his wackier digressions, but this soon yields diminishing results, because it's impossible to understand how some of his meanderings could possibly be credited by a rational human being, let alone how they could impel people to suffer and die in their defence. At this point, one throws up one's hands, and mutters something along the lines of: "Well, a hundred million Chinese can't be wrong." But such a reaction offers scant comfort, and does not advance the plot.

Li is well aware of the value of sacred (and profane) texts, having come of age during the Cultural Revolution, during which Chairman Mao's *Little Red Book* functioned as the blueprint for Communism's true believers. Much of the material that follows is contained in *China Falun Gong*, Li's first book. It is a strange piece of work, and readers might wish to consult it, if it's commercially available in their area. Readers should not, however, expect that they'll be able to tell the players, even with a program in hand. As an illustration, here are two question-and-answers, taken directly from the text. Both deal with the pivotal falun, or rotating wheel.

Q: How did I come to have Falun on?

A: You did not have it on. I released Falun and planted it in your lower abdomen. Of course, this is not done in this physical space, but in another space. Otherwise, with the intestines in your belly, how could you bear it when it turns? Falun exists in another space, having nothing to do with this world.

Q: What does Falun look like?

A: We can only say that Falun is almost golden yellow, because there is no such colour in our space. Its background is bright red, and the background of its outer circle is orange. The two Taiji Patterns composed of red and black fish belong to the Tao School, while the other two in red and blue belong to the Great Way School. So they are not the same. The sign [a swastika] is golden yellow. A person with his Celestial Eye open on a low plane will find it rotating like an electric fan. If he can see it clearly, he will find that it is very beautiful, and it is always an inspiration and encouragement to a practitioner on his way towards cultivation.

Further verbatim quotes, devoid of commentary or explanation, would be superfluous. But now that readers have a taste of what they're in for, we can proceed, to see where Li's writings lead us.

The Roots of Falun Gong

*L*i knows his history and, in cobbling together his admixture of Buddhism, Taoism, and Confucianism, was aware that over the centuries Buddhism played an integral role in China's times of national crises. When the Han dynasty fell in the third century, Chinese intellectuals and members of the upper classes, followed by common men and women, turned to Buddhism in an attempt to explain this terrible turn of events.

The collapse of that once mighty dynasty (which was contemporary with, but more extensive than, the Roman Empire) seemed to bear out the Buddha's first truth, which holds that all is suffering. The Buddha's rational examination of suffering's origins became an integral part of this painful period of self-examination in China's history. Added to this was the Buddhist idea that salvation is available to everyone, even the most miserable member of society. This struck the Chinese as an entirely revolutionary idea, and brought new hope and comfort to the less fortunate.

As well, people were looking for protection in the face of massive social change. Benevolent gods were conspicuous in their absence from Confucianism, which was rarefied and stand-offish, but Buddhism offered a rich assortment of deities. All it took was prayer, and a bodhisattva (or enlightened being) would spring to the assistance of a troubled believer. Nor did Buddhism shy away from spiritual show business. Dramatic depictions of multi-layered heavens and hells give the Chinese a dramatic and graphic impetus to lead moral lives amidst day-to-day chaos.

Hence, Li's wholesale appropriation of Buddhist imagery to bolster his initial teachings. In *China Falun Gong*, he makes 124 direct references to Buddhism, but only seven to Confucianism, and a scant two to Taoism.

The book opens soberly enough with a photograph of Li, nattily dressed in a blue blazer and crisp white shirt. He wears a green tartan tie with a horse-and-rider motif. His face is without wrinkles, round and soft. The corners of his lips seem on the brink of arching into a tentative smile, but his gaze is more contemplative than friendly, more curious than warm.

The next page contains a colourful diagram — actually a constellation of symbols that describes the union of the two most influential religious systems in Chinese history. At the centre of the sacred cosmos burns a golden Buddhist svastikam, or swastika, an almost universal "wheel of light," around which orbit eight celestial bodies in the shape of four smaller swastikas and four Taoist yin-yangs. But, as stated, Li soon proceeds to zero in on Buddhism's philosophical imagery and philosophical principles. At times, he denounces Buddhist teachings as worthless compared to his own, then, on the next page, employs them when he needs a voice of authority to shore up the occasionally thin-sounding lessons of Falun Gong.

In the Beginning There Was Qi

Li constantly asserts that the task of acquiring real and powerful self-transformation begins with the skillful manipulation of the primal energy that the Chinese have for thousands of years referred to as qi. We touched upon qi in Chapter One, while looking at qigong systems. The historian Stephen F. Teiser, in *Religions of China in Practice*, explains that "Everything that ever existed, at all times, is made of qi." This includes "inanimate matter, humans and animals, the sky, ideas and emotions, demons and ghosts." Qi is therefore both psychological — connected to human thoughts and feelings — and physical. Teiser translates it as "psychophysical stuff," or, simply put, mind and body linked by a mighty life force.

This sounds daunting, but in fact the West has become increasingly receptive to such notions. Many people see virtue in a holistic approach to mind and body. Despite its indisputable successes, the highly compartmentalized approach adopted by Western medicine leaves many patients unsatisfied, searching for something more. They instinctively understand that physical and mental health are inexorably linked. If Westerners are willing to give this sort of thing a hearing, imagine its impact on the Chinese. That is why Li started the ball rolling by presenting Falun Gong as a "high order of qigong," one that would be capable of tapping into the unlimited potential of the human mind (which Jung refers to as "the most powerful weapon ever devised by nature") in an effort to heal or improve his practitioners' physical condition.

Of course, Li's "Great Cultivation Law" of that high order is a system of his own devising — but he assures us that the powers he cultivates, far from being inaccessible or arcane, are in fact internationally available: "The practice of qigong is not found in China alone . . . In some Western countries, it is called magic art." At a low level, he says, qigong can be used to "exhibit miracles" and for entertainment. He then inserts a peculiar anecdote concerning the professional magician David Copperfield, who, Li seems to indicate, did indeed walk through the Great Wall of China; it wasn't an illusion. Returning almost immediately to more elevated themes, however, Li adds that qigong serves far nobler purposes. It can be used to cure disease, and to "cultivate one's Benti," or true being.

Li knows all too well that the idea of qi came to the fore of Chinese philosophy in the second century, when Taoism reasserted the importance of the individual and the necessity of connection with the natural world, as opposed to Confucianism's obsessive insistence on hierarchy, moral codes, and rote obedience. Taoists developed the idea of wu wei (pronounced woo-way), or non-action, which in fact does not mean passivity. Rather, it means behaving naturally and without social artifice, thus allowing the law of Tao (the "way of nature and the universe") to act through us, in turn ensuring correct conduct.

This concept was not confined to the Orient. It found an expression in Rousseau's insistence that only the natural and primitive could save mankind from the corrupting power of social institutions. In China, though, the Taoists sought, not the naivety, but the spiritual honesty of a child. They longed to return to a closer unity with nature, to a distant past that existed before borders, empires, social classes, and crushing bureaucracies. All these, they said, were aberrations that dragged people away from a harmonious relationship with the natural world, through which flowed the vital essence of qi.

Li's concept of a sufficiently cultivated qi is in line with this thinking. He defines it as "cosmic energy, the formless and invisible matter in the universe," which can nonetheless be tapped into so as to "dispel diseases and improve physical conditions." In this hope he is not alone. Historically, many Chinese medical practitioners have hoped to manipulate qi. Acupuncturists, for example, maintain that qi circulates through fourteen channels, called meridians, that have branches connected to bodily organs. If qi is blocked, sickness will follow. The trick is to unblock it by whatever means necessary — be it through acupuncture or by performing tai-chi-like exercises — and thus return the body to a natural, healthy balance.

The idea that one can achieve equilibrium by means of accessing a mysterious, vital substance is by no means unique to Chinese medical history. Western healers struggled for centuries with similar propositions, such as the theory of the four humours, identified as blood, yellow bile, black bile, and phlegm. (Bear this in mind when you are tempted to write off Li's idea of karma — a black substance — and de — a milky white one). Galen, the famous Greek physician, argued for these humours in the second century, maintaining that they had to exist in a delicate balance in order for one to enjoy good health. Any disequilibrium, Galen said, could lead to disease, madness, or both. His teachings formed the theoretical foundation for all Western medical training until the 1850s.

The trouble is that no one has ever tracked qi to its lair. It does not lend itself to a control experiment. The ancient Chinese practitioners arrived at the body's 365 acupuncture points, not by means of anatomical knowledge, but because there were 365 days in the year. Contemporary acupuncturists insist that the number of points is in fact closer to 2,000, leading critics to wonder if there are any spots on the body that don't qualify. Meanwhile, researchers have shown that the mild analgesic effect created by the insertion of an acupuncture needle can be reproduced by simply pinching the skin.

Besides, as pointed out by Dr. Stephen Basser in a study titled *Acupuncture, The Facts*, acupuncture and other Eastern nostrums "arose at a time when there was no understanding of modern physiology, biochemistry, or healing mechanisms." If a sick person was stuck full of needles and then got better, "it was assumed that the treatment had caused the improvement. There was no formal study of diseases and their natural history, and no attempt was made to determine whether improvement would have occurred without the treatment." In sum, Eastern wisdom may not be able to offer up a sure-fire cure for every ill.

In the words of the philosopher Denis Diderot, "What has not been examined impartially, has not been well examined; skepticism is therefore the first step toward truth." This questing spirit produced the Enlightenment, which swept eighteenth-century Europe, and in the process, swept Galen's four humours out of the operating room. But that same spirit did not take hold in China until very recent times. Today, despite decades of Communist Party support for acupuncture and other traditional remedies, Western medicine is by far the more widely accepted. Of forty-six major medical journals published by the Chinese Medical Association, not one is devoted to the benefits of needles and pins. Elsewhere in Asia, particularly in Japan, acupuncture has all but disappeared; whatever growth it enjoys is occurring almost exclusively in the West.

But qi retains its popularity, despite all manner of strange and wonderful claims. Li and other qigong masters maintain that they can channel their personal qi to cure disease, make water sweet, bend spoons, open the celestial eye, and send disciples flying across the room. No such claim has ever been proven in the context of a controlled experiment. On the contrary, whenever experiments have been conducted, they've without exception proven to be embarrassing failures for the qigong gurus involved.

Despite numerous studies, Western scientists have failed to uncover hard evidence of the mysterious "meridians," or of qi itself. Still Li asserts that by cultivating one's qi, "the molecular components of one's body are transformed into high energy matter." He also says that "Qigong can put an end to disease once and for all." Suffice it to say that, for our purposes here, the idea of qi serves best as a philosophical point of departure — a metaphor for a no-doubt desirable end that could be achieved by more sensible means — rather than as an identifiable force or physical presence.

Master Li's Law Bodies

*A*ny true believer needs to think that his or her faith will not only mend spiritual ills and guarantee a place in the great beyond, but will also provide everyday necessities. This desire accounts for an equally universal plethora of magic and miracles on demand.

And once again, it's an easy concept to deride, but here we are on thin ice. In North America, televangelists exhort cancer patients to press their hands to the screen, in the desperate hope of a cure. In China, meanwhile, pathogen-causing malevolent spirits are still abroad in the land (or at least in the forefront of the public's imagination), and are combatted by practitioners of the Buddhist occult. A belief in faith healing was not an original teaching of either Christ or the Buddha, but a change imposed on their original doctrines by the very real needs of lay people.

This passionate hope that health, wealth, and even more remarkable attributes may be acquired by signing up for a given belief system does much to explain Li's promise to endow Falun Gong practitioners with "supernormal" powers. These include the abilities to travel psychically, to pull down large buildings, to remain dry in a downpour, to see through walls and into one's own body by means of the celestial eye, to glimpse events taking place far away by means of "Remote Sight," and, indeed, to perceive what's happening in other dimensions.

"Human beings," writes Li, "only know the space in which we dwell . . . as for other spaces, we qigong masters have already perceived dozens of them, which can be explained in theory but cannot yet be proven by science . . . For instance, there is a place called the Bermuda Islands, also known as the Triangle of Demons. Some ships and planes disappeared there, but reappeared some years later. Nobody has given a satisfactory explanation to this phenomenon, because we cannot break through the theoretical framework shaped by the human mind." Unless, of course, we fasten our seatbelts and go along for the bumpy ride offered by Master Li.

Perhaps the most imperative power (by his telling) at Li's command is his ability to protect Falun Gong practitioners from disease not only through qigong exercises, but also by psychically endowing them with one or more "law bodies." These are not to be confused with the spinning falun, which is psychically planted in their abdomens — really, no more far-fetched than being imbued with the powers of the Holy Spirit.

But despite their powers, the law bodies have a sort of shelf life, and are good only for as long as practitioners remain loyal to Li. As in any faith, membership has its privileges, which can be revoked if one backslides. "Each of you has at least one of my Law Bodies on condition that you are a practitioner of Falun Gong," Li warns. "If you are not, of course, my Law Body will not take care of you. It won't even if I ask it to, for it knows everything you are thinking about."

And what if you fall ill, even though you have received a law body and are still a Falun Gong member in good standing? It comes as no surprise that Li has an explanation: "No disease is allowed to attack you after a period of time. If you have an illness again, something like a cold or a stomach-ache, it is not a disease. It is a tribulation you need to deal with." In other words, you have unfinished karmic business that the law bodies cannot or will not address.

The root cause of all disease, according to Li, is an "evil spirit found in another space." The rotating falun cures disease by sending the spirit packing, but Li also admonishes us to be on guard against animal spirits, who "want to possess a human body in order to consume the essence out of it."

Nor should a practitioner be seduced by initial gains that may be achieved while under the spell of such a spirit. Li warns that "They will satisfy your desire for personal fame and gain and will make you rich and famous. But they will not help you for nothing . . . When they leave you, you will have nothing left and become very weak or simply turn into a vegetable man."

Falun Gong and Taoist Immortality

*L*i intuitively understands that it's not enough to facilitate his followers' ascent into the "Falun Paradise," where "the great enlightened people stay," or even to augment their purely spiritual advance here on this earthly plane. Both Buddhism and Falun Gong are essentially anti-materialistic, but both bend the rules, pledging tangible rewards as well. Yet Li's promise to fulfil mundane desires is more than an attempt to cover all the spiritual bases. Rather, it's a claim built on Taoism, another of his borrowing points.

Taoism is and always will be an earthly religion that reflects the Chinese love of nature and their belief that this world, these flesh-and-blood bodies, are worth the candle. A Taoist monk may indeed retreat to the mountaintop, never to be seen again, but it's not because he wishes to escape entirely the vale of tears below. Rather, he is like Thomas Jefferson, building his dream home high on a Virginia hill and urging the United States to cherish agrarianism. The Taoist wishes to live honestly with nature, away from the corrupting influence of civilization. This is a far cry from the rejection of life itself. In fact, so life-affirming is the Taoist outlook that priests sought (and still seek) to extend their time on earth by means of the alchemical production of the elixir of immortality.

Li is quite in tune with this thinking. He plucked from Buddhism the ideas of karma and hell, but all his teachings are centred not upon some imagined future life in paradise or torment, but on self-transformation in the present tense.

That is why, in the chapter of *China Falun Gong* entitled Change of Benti, he promises that Falun Gong will fight off the ravages of aging and possibly conquer death itself: "Practitioners find that through practice the wrinkles on their faces have become fewer, their cheeks are glowing with health, and their bodies are becoming so light that they do not feel tired when walking or working." Li explains that he himself offers living proof of the efficacy of these measures: Thanks to the powers of his personal falun, he has remained physically unchanged for the last twenty years. Others can follow in his footsteps. A sufficiently disciplined practitioner, he adds, will free himself "from the control of the five elements [water, fire, metal, wood, and soil], and acquire a body composed of the matter from the other spaces." At that point, he "will not be subject to the restriction of time of our space, and will stay young forever."

How has Li located the elusive garden of eternal youth? It's all explainable, he says, in scientific terms. Falun Gong makes "a fundamental change of the molecular composition of the human body, stores the collected matter of high energy in each cell, and finally replaces the composition of the cell with the matter of high energy. Then there is no more metabolism."

Outer and Inner Alchemy

$\mathcal{M}$any of us would recoil from the above claims, but it is within the bounds of possibility that Li's teachings may produce a certain peace of mind that, coupled with no-doubt beneficial exercises, could bring new vigour to Falun Gong practitioners' bodies. And, a belief in the possibility of immortality is nothing new.

Mao Zedong, the father of the Communist Party, was given to writing poetry in his spare moments. In one verse, he refers sadly to the death of his wife, Yang, at the hands of the Nationalist government in 1933, but comforts himself with the thought that she "floated up" to other spheres, and was "given to drink of gold cassia wine" — in other words, an immortality elixir. Mao went on to express the wistful hope that she might remain alive in a better, far-off realm. In fact, he seems to have been much concerned with such thoughts. Julia Ching, in her book *Chinese Religions*, discloses that the beginning of the Cultural Revolution coincided with Mao's displeasure at the production of a play that he considered had criticized him for, among other things, seeking to "live forever."

In fairness, Li's techniques seem relatively harmless when compared with the methods employed by Taoist priests in their search for the elixir of immortality.

The priests conducted this search, as noted earlier, by alchemical means. Unlike European alchemists, they did not wish to convert base metals into gold. They did in fact experiment with metals, but as part of a process known as Outer Alchemy, which they hoped would result in a Methuselah-like lifespan. Sadly, these concoctions often sped the demise of those who sipped, swallowed, and sucked them, since they typically contained massive quantities of cinnabar (or mercuric sulphide) and lead.

Oddly enough, these noxious compounds sometimes coagulated into large clumps of mercury located deep in their victims' bowels, which effectively pickled their corpses. In a sense, then, they did achieve their aim of preserving the body for all eternity — they left us with forensic evidence of what polished them off. Li seems to be alluding to this phenomenon when he remarks that, "At the cremation of their bodies after death, relics are found, which are so solid and pretty that even modern scientific instruments cannot make out what they are made up of."

In any event, because of the demonstrably lethal effects of Outer Alchemy, many Taoists turned instead to a safer form — in essence, the cultivation of qi to achieve longevity, if not outright immortality. These attempts were termed Inner Alchemy, and were seized upon by Li. The idea here is that meditative techniques can cultivate qi and conduct it through the body, thus developing an "inner elixir."

According to Isabelle Robinette in her book *Taoism: Growth of a Religion*, Inner Alchemy is experiencing a revival in China, based on a repository of lore passed down unchanged in an unbroken chain for millennia. These techniques are exceedingly arcane, and far more heavily laden with cosmological, spiritual, and intellectual components than the relatively simple techniques that mark garden-variety qigong.

Li claims, of course, that "the cultivation way of Falun Gong is completely different" from these practices, but there are, in fact, striking similarities.

Traditionally, most Inner Alchemy meditation techniques break the body down into three fields — the head, chest, and abdomen — through which the meditator is taught to conduct qi into what he visualizes as a microcosmic orbit. This sounds almost exactly like Li's falun, whose purpose is to "draw inward a great amount of qi." The difference, according to Li, is that the devotee of traditional Inner Alchemy must *work at* drawing qi through "cinnabar fields," whereas in Falun Gong, this happens automatically.

What benefits may be derived from meditation based on this philosophy? Elsewhere in *Chinese Religions*, Julia Ching explains that qigong practitioners employ a mix of exercises and meditation techniques so as to "empty the heart" and achieve an "interior, ecstatic vision" that will both ward off sickness and evil spirits and lead, under optimum circumstances, to immortality.

Li goes along with that with his insistence that "Qigong can put an end to disease once and for all." But a problem arises, and Li does not shrink from it. He admits that, while Falun Gong can cure disease in individuals, a mysterious "natural law" prevents it from being used on a larger scale. In other words, each practitioner is on his or her own.

Li notes how qigong's curative effectiveness dropped "sharply" when it became institutionalized — that is, when official, government-sanctioned qigong hospitals and clinics were established. This unhappy turn of events led him to conclude that we cannot "use the supernormal law to replace the normal function of ordinary human society."

Li knows his true calling, if not his limitations, as he reveals in an unusually telling passage. "I came into public not to treat diseases," he writes. "There are people who are destined to suffer from diseases . . . we treat patients in an organized way for the purpose of giving publicity to our cultivation system. As I have just come into public and enjoy little popularity, people are not likely to attend the classes I hold to import my cultivation system if we cannot convince them of the efficacy of our system by treating diseases and giving advice. We have done so for the publicity of our cultivation system, not for the treatment itself."

The Cultivation of Xinxing

*A*s for xinxing — a combination of moral virtuousness and the relinquishing of all evil thoughts and improper conduct — Li announces that practitioners must grant its cultivation "first priority." As explained earlier, xinxing includes a person's attitude towards what Li refers to as "cosmic qualities": the moral trinity known as Zhen (Truth), Shan (Compassion), and Ren (Forbearance).

Li's commitment to Truth has its origins in the Taoist insistence on naturalness of action and his identification of Compassion in Buddhist thought. Ren, however, appears — at least on the surface — to be an idea based on the humanist teachings of Confucius. But there's an important difference. Confucian Ren is similar to the Christian emphasis on charity, and describes the quality of benevolence and good-heartedness that a Confucian must exhibit to everyone, regardless of social rank. Li's interpretation of Ren goes much further, by incorporating the Buddhist spirit of tolerance and non-violence, even in the face of terrible abuse. Nowhere is this more evident than when Li's practitioners refuse to resist as security police drag them away. This is in keeping with Li's view. "When an ordinary person suffers humiliation," he writes, "he will draw his sword to fight, open his mouth to curse, or raise his fist to punch . . . As a cultivator, you should be not only tolerant of and patient towards, but also grateful to, the person who contradicts or humiliates you to your face." In other words, such a person presents, by his actions, a tribulation that must be met with forbearance.

Master Li and the Cravings of the Body and the Mind

*L*i repeats many times throughout the two-hundred-odd pages of *China Falun Gong* the need to tame sensual impulses. In the chapter entitled Abolishing Attachments, he insists that practitioners who wish to attain "emptiness" and continue to be counted as his disciples have a duty to destroy all their material "attachments" and to abandon all that is dear to them, thus eliminating destructive human "cravings."

These concepts are Buddhist in origin. In other words, they are not inherently Chinese. Rather, they were introduced to China by wandering Buddhist monks in the first century after the birth of Christ. To understand Li's concern with "emptiness" and "cravings" and his overriding preoccupation with "attachments" of every kind, we must turn for a moment to his source material — the very heart of Buddhist thought, which is known as Dependent Origination and the Four Noble Truths.

"Before you get enlightened," Li says, "you simply judge the right and wrongs of a matter by the criterion of the worldly law. You are not able to see the truth of it and the causational relationship behind it. It is because of causality that one beats, curses or bullies another person."

Here, Li is at one with the Buddha, who said that the key to understanding the nature of existence was to perceive a concept called Dependent Origination, meaning simply that no entity or happening appears by itself, out of the ether. Everything that exists does so because of an interaction of various conditions. When the conditions disappear, so does the thing or event.

At the time, this was a truly revolutionary assertion, but the Buddha applied it to all points of the moral compass. He explained, for example, that society creates criminals. Thus, a miscreant was not a monster, but the product (the cause-and-effect consequence) of numerous factors operative within a particular community. When the adverse circumstances that drove a person to a life of crime (unemployment, racism, hopelessness, or poverty) were removed, he or she would return to the straight and narrow.

The Buddha's theory embraced both criminals and eternal entities such as a creator-God and everlasting souls. It may strike Westerners as strange that Buddhists believe in the transmigration of souls, but Buddhists look just as dubiously at the Christian belief that a single deity was responsible for the universe. Indeed, Buddhists deny God's existence, which for them is not supported by logic and experience.

At any rate, Dependent Origination sounds quite in line with the latest thinking. As Ninian Smart points out in *Beyond Ideology*, "One of the main attractions of Buddhism is the modernity of its ideas . . . in reducing the visible world to a vast interconnected swarm of events, it echoes the findings of modern science . . . It seems not to have those clashes between the spiritual and the scientific which have seemed to plague Western faith."

To take the Buddha's, and Li's, thinking a step further, it therefore follows that if everything depends on an infinite number of temporary and fluctuating conditions, nothing at all can be said to have an essential eternal identity. This conclusion has a huge effect on how we view the world. If the Buddha and Li are right, the names we give to things and situations, people and places, become mere labels of convenience that describe only what we perceive as their true nature. In reality, as both the Buddha and Li insist, there is only emptiness. But that doesn't mean that nothing exists. In the words of the Dalai Lama, "Things do exist, but they do not have an independent, autonomous reality." It is in this sense that all things are "empty," and no person, place, or thing can be wholly good or wholly evil.

In the doctrine of Dependent Origination, all of our thoughts, emotions, and behaviour hinge in turn on other factors. Every day, our positive or negative actions, emotions, and attitudes bear either sweet or bitter fruit. The opening stanzas of the *Dhammapada*, an ancient anthology of Buddhist sayings, express beautifully this idea: "What we are today flows from our thoughts of yesterday. Our present thoughts determine our life of tomorrow. Our life is the creation of our mind. If a man speaks or acts with an impure mind, then suffering follows him."

Thus, everything that happens to us happens for a reason. Unhappy outcomes aren't necessarily our fault, but the Buddha urges us to scour our lives, actions, and environment for a rational explanation of any predicament. In the Buddhist vision of the world, there's very little room for chance, bad luck, or divine intervention.

We have explored this at some length because it leads us directly to both Li Hongzhi's Buddhist-inspired warnings against "attachments" of every kind, and to the very bedrock of Buddhist thought, the Four Noble Truths.

The Four Noble Truths

The aim of Western psychotherapy is to cure patients of their personal delusions, alleviating their fears and moderating their desires so that they may once again enter "normal" society — sharing, a cynic would remark, in its collective delusion. But Buddhism and Falun Gong do not propose to do so. Their aim is not to tinker with these attitudes and behaviours, but to annihilate them at their very roots. This is the path that leads to Nirvana (in Buddhism, a departure from the human world by completing the process of cultivation), a path that begins with the Four Noble Truths.

"When sitting in practice," remarks Li, "many practitioners shed tears for no reason. Whatever they think about, they feel sad. Whoever they see, they see his sufferings. This indicates that their compassion is developing and that their nature and true self have begun to communicate with Zhen-Shan-Ren."

At this stage, Li's followers have begun to grasp the First Noble Truth, which states that to live in this world, and in an impermanent body prone to sickness, disease, and grief, is to suffer. Whether that suffering is obvious and physical, or psychic and hidden behind a mask of feigned contentment, pain is our constant lot, an inescapable part of being human.

This proposition is difficult for Westerners to accept. Surely everyone aspires and strives to be happy. We look around and feel that life is all right, that things could be worse, and that, on balance, we're doing well. But most of us have to make a conscious effort to seek out the hopeful and to avoid the ugly and painful. We accentuate the positive, in part, out of self-preservation. The dark side beckons, and we might succumb to despair if forced to contemplate the terrifying duality of the world as it really is, composed of equal parts pleasure and agony. But, by emphasizing the good and dismissing suffering as aberrant, most of us live, as Edward Conze writes in *Buddhism: Its Essence and Development*, "in a fool's paradise."

Conze adds that, "As subjects of conversation, distressing and disheartening aspects of life shock the 'nice people' and frighten the others." The Buddha and Li, however, do not shrink from life's downside. Both confront it head-on, not out of a nihilistic urge to make people's flesh creep, but because they believe that they have the cure. Buddhists are expected to leave behind the self-centred obsession with searching out only the good and pleasurable while ignoring distress, just as Falun Gong practitioners find that in the discomfort of "the other," they will come to understand their own pain. By extending their comprehension of the agony visited upon all living things, they begin to chip away at the citadel of the ego and dampen the delusional craving for permanent happiness in a hopelessly transient world.

The need to understand the suffering around us also leads to the doctrine of non-violence or "no-harming," in which all life is held to be sacred, and the killing of any being, even in war or for food, is strictly off-limits. The doctrine of no-harming also forces us to deal with the fact that the acts we find pleasurable may increase the suffering of other creatures. Eating meat can be enjoyed only if we avoid all thought of the feelings of the animal that's butchered to grace our table.

Both the Buddha and Li abhor the killing of animals, but Li goes further, insisting that plant life is equally sacred. He denounces the thoughtless destruction of innocent flora by unscrupulous qigong practitioners who roll about on top of it in efforts to absorb its life force. This, he remarks, "is a karma-accumulating act. It is also killing. Modern science has proven that the plant has not only life, but also intelligence, mind and feelings, even the function of supernormal sense."

The Buddha and Li are reminding us that, deep down, some part of our unconscious is probably already disturbed by the moral implications of taking life, of eating the flesh of another being while, outside the restaurant, someone lies on a sleeping bag atop a subway grate. As we'll see in a moment, when we examine Falun Gong's view of karma, no-harming is an area of consciousness that both Chinese and Western minds would do well to focus on.

Buddhism's Second Noble Truth is that suffering is caused by cravings of every kind. This, as we have seen, squares with Li's denunciation of "attachments."

The Buddha states, and Li agrees, that the "Five Aggregates" — material, feelings, perceptions, impulses, and consciousness — all feed an incessant hunger for sensation, pleasure, and reward.

If we're human, we are subject to a vast array of sense desires. Li would like to jettison them all, for he deems them to be the source of all our pain.

Everything qualifies; everything to Li is an attachment. In another of *China Falun Gong*'s question-and-answer sessions, he responds to the suggestion that it's indispensable to have sex, as follows: "Sex is a desire of ordinary people. We practitioners should let go of it and take it lightly."

Falun Gong thus joins Buddhism in seeking to conquer the "savage master" of the libido, as well as another and almost as powerful desire — the urge to consume. "It is difficult for a non-practitioner to find himself satisfied," Li writes. "He wants everything except the stones on the ground."

Li put forward this view from the very first, which ought to have landed him in hot water with the authorities sooner than he did. Even in the early 1990s, the Chinese government was frantically re-tooling antediluvian industries in preparation for a Red Capitalist tomorrow, placing the Chinese people under new pressures to buy as never before. And there was Li, swimming against the materialist tide. "What others want I do not want," he wrote. "What others have I do not have. What the ordinary people strive for or the small profit they have obtained is only transient . . . You can take nothing away at death, though you are a millionaire or a high-ranking official."

All that having been said, neither the Buddha nor Li deny that the senses bring pleasure. It's the *craving* for pleasure that must be guarded against. Li's insistence that his practitioners live "in the world" strikes a middle ground. Many material things, a beautiful body, a wonderful novel, a house by the sea, produce the most intense gratification. And all these can be enjoyed — as long as they're part of a reward system to help us along the arduous path to enlightenment, in the full knowledge that any happiness we derive from them will be ephemeral. An object that once brought its owner fulfilment might one day inspire boredom or frustration. This holds true in friendships and sexual relationships as well. Passion can turn to revulsion, kinship to mistrust. "If you look carefully," warns the Dalai Lama, "everything that we consider desirable brings us suffering in the end."

Buddhism's panoply of gods reflects this bleak reality. At first glance they appear similar to the deities that reigned atop Mount Olympus — but with the difference that even they are not immortal. Like their human counterparts, they too are condemned to suffering, death, and decay.

This leads us to the Third Noble Truth, which speaks to the cessation of pain. The Buddha taught that torment will end only if we cast off each and every remainder of our cravings — a process of release, forsaking, abandonment, and (he too uses the phrase) non-attachment. Li cautions a practitioner to "treat all material concerns very, very casually, crave for nothing and let things go their own way. Only by doing so can he free himself from attachments."

But this "cessation" of cravings does not mean the violent and abrupt suppression of desires and passions. Rather, it ought to be a gradual process of pacification that leads, not to a tight-lipped and sweaty denial of sensuality, but to its own particular bliss. Like a stone in the river, life's pains and pleasures sweep up against you, swirling and boiling around you. You feel the current, sometimes swift and cold, now gentle and warm. But you're never carried downstream in its grasp; you remain fast, unmoved. As the *Dhammapada* puts it: "Sorry is he whose burden is heavy, and happy is he who has cast it down. When once he has cast off his burden, he will seek to be burdened no more."

The Fourth Noble Truth, also known as the Eight-Fold Path, points the way to Nirvana. This truth is composed of eight mini-truths: Right View, Right Intention, Right Speech, Right Discipline, Right Livelihood, Right Effort, Right Mindfulness, and Right Concentration. Li has put his own spin on all these components.

Right View is akin to Socrates' statement that only the examined life is worth living, and once again cautions against confusion caused by the immediate senses. To guard against this, we're urged to develop our powers of critical thinking and avoid pre-judging people or situations. As noted by the celebrated Buddhist teacher Chogyam Trungpa in his book entitled *The Myth of Freedom and the Way of Meditation*, even the terms "friend" and "enemy" can lead to ruin. They are nothing but labels, and by imposing them on a given situation, we can come to grief. Much better, according to Trungpa, to consider each moment "as if it were newly born."

Li's take is that "you may get so angry that you feel very uncomfortable and painful here and there in your body. However, you did not flare up, but managed to restrain yourself. This is good because you begin to endure, to exercise forbearance intentionally."

Right View also embraces various dos and don'ts. Killing, stealing, lying, and so on are out. Truth is in. The search for truth will give you the ultimate in self-defence.

The second and third points, Right Intention and Right Speech, are closely related. Both Buddhism and Falun Gong urge us to be straightforward and honest in word and deed, meeting life head-on and using direct, expressive language that conveys exactly what we mean and feel.

Right Discipline again preaches the power of simplicity. Constant self-examination results in an uncomplicated life. Li urges the same honesty when investigating the causes of our personal misfortunes. "If every one of us cultivates the inner self," he writes, "no one will need to be governed, as everyone will discipline himself or herself."

Right Livelihood suggests a life of moderation, a middle path between wealth and poverty, and cautions against a withdrawal from society or an indulgence in extreme forms of asceticism. It recognizes the necessity of work, but stresses that money won't buy happiness. As stated earlier, Li teaches that people who work hard and treat others fairly deserve the fruits of their labours. "It does not matter how high your position ranks, or how much wealth you own," he says. "The key is whether you can abandon that attachment."

Right Effort exhorts us to be fully aware in all situations, embracing all sorts of endeavours with equal zeal. "You deserve to earn more money if you make more effort," writes Li. "That is because you are rewarded for the effort you have put in among everyday people." But Right Effort also means that we must first decide which endeavours warrant intense dedication. To do so, it's necessary to "be present," to focus on worthwhile ends and avoid getting bogged down in fruitless inner debate.

Right Mindfulness is the thoughtful examination of every moment with a view to achieving a level of calm, and making sure that every action counts; while Right Concentration refers to meditation (Li's "clean and clear mind"), which finds its zenith in yoga, a discipline that combines absolute mastery of the body with dominance of the mind. Only now are Western science and thought beginning to treat the two as one. In the East, they've always been inseparable.

Falun Gong and Meditation

How does Falun Gong direct its practitioners to meditate? Li is adamant that the perfection of inner tranquillity is vital, and shares the view that meditation is not a philosophy, but a skill to be practised and mastered by first crushing or screening out all extraneous sensory input.

He cites first the distractions of the flesh, warning that

"another form of interference comes from the demons of lust. When sitting in practice or dreaming, a handsome man or a beautiful woman may appear before you, trying to attract and seduce you . . . The test is so difficult to pass that many practitioners have failed. This is a great test which you must pass. Otherwise, you will not achieve the Way and attain perfection in your cultivation."

But, having passed the test, says Li, adepts can "become tranquil as soon as they sit down," indicating that they've reached "high-level cultivation." Li encourages the falterers, noting that "it doesn't matter if you cannot achieve tranquillity for the time being," because "you can gradually manage to do so." In other words, practice makes perfect. Other than this, at least in his published writings, Li is uncustomarily reticent when it comes to meditative techniques, insisting that the beginner cannot achieve inner peace through "tricks," but only by first extinguishing all attachments, examining the self, and "working on your heart."

Nonetheless, Li's approach to meditation is probably akin to the one summarized by David J. Kalupahana, who describes it in his book *Buddhist Philosophy: A Historical Analysis* as beginning with a practitioner focusing all his powers of attention on some object, and achieving the first stage of trance when he's able to subdue dangerous urges such as "sense desire, ill-will, sloth and torpor, excitedness and perplexity."

Next, one silences one's frenetic inner dialogue and is imbued with a sense of confidence and peace. But this itself "is a hindrance to peace of mind," and must be overcome in the third and fourth stages, during which even feelings of elation are extinguished, and the consciousness is "made supple and receptive and can be directed toward even higher stages." These are the so-called formless jhanas, which eventually entail a state where there's no such thing as perception and non-perception.

No discussion of the importance of meditation to Falun Gong could be complete without reference to Ch'an (or, in Japanese, Zen), the one true Chinese Buddhist school. This tradition, to which Li owes the bulk of his meditational teachings, is also the one he criticizes most energetically. In his words, "Zen Buddhism has reached the dead end of the bull's horn, and there is no longer anything to teach."

Li continues in much the same vein for three solid pages of *China Falun Gong*, but muddies his argument by quoting extensively from the Buddha, in an effort to argue for achieving enlightenment by means of classical Buddhist or Falun Gong–style formal instruction.

At first, his attack on Zen seems pointless as well as hyperbolic, until we realize that, according to Zen belief, teachers such as Li, who spread their doctrines by lecturing endlessly and churning out publications by the score, are serving only to obscure true enlightenment. In Ch'an teaching, Li's intellectual approach is doomed. Enlightenment cannot be planned for as one does a holiday, or saved up for like putting money aside for a new car. It can take place a minute from now, or never. Longing for it is only another attachment, and will further block its occurrence, as will rational contemplation, such as studying scripture, or — more particularly — Li's books. Both will inhibit "direct seeing" into the heart.

A Zen believer would dismiss Li's writings (indeed, his entire methodology) as mere "head knowledge." As Li says, Zen Buddhism maintains that "Fa should not be taught, that Fa is not Fa if it is taught, and that there is no teachable Fa." Rather, it holds that "one can only understand something via heart and soul." If so, many of Li's activities fall by the wayside.

Even while Li attacks Zen, he recognizes the position that its founder, Bodhidharma, occupies in the Chinese consciousness. This is because it was only with the creation of the Ch'an school that Buddhism, a late-blooming import from India, managed to integrate itself into Chinese culture.

By the seventh century, Buddhism had been practised in China for about six hundred years, but with limited success. At first, the Chinese had been dazzled and captivated, enthralled and at times terrified by the Buddhist vision of multi-layered heavens and hells. Later, however, they began to wonder whether they should bring Buddhism down to earth, in keeping with their practical nature. At this time, they settled on meditation. Here was a pragmatic skill that, with disciplined study, could be developed to yield positive results in this lifetime, never mind the next.

Indeed, adherents of the Ch'an school aspire to no-beating-around-the-bush Instant Enlightenment. This emphasis on spontaneity came about through a cross-pollination with Taoism's devotion to naturalness of action. And, being an attractive prospect, Li added it to the mix of beliefs that formed the basis of Falun Gong — although he typically refuses to credit the source.

"The practitioner's celestial eye," Li writes, "is instantly opened to the highest plane. He can communicate with intelligent beings in other spaces, see the true picture of all the spaces and individual paradises of the cosmos all at once, and display his supernatural powers. Immediate enlightenment is most difficult to achieve. Through the ages, only a man of very good inborn quality is selected as a disciple, and the cultivation system is handed down from one to another singly, for ordinary people just cannot endure it. I have, however, attained immediate enlightenment in that way."

Good for Li — but in claiming that "ordinary people" cannot do likewise, he is in conflict with Zen tradition, which teaches that everyone has the potential for instant enlightenment. This is good news, and far easier than developing one's Buddha nature (or true self) through poring over scriptures (which were so disdained by Zen monks that they kept them in the lavatory) or engaging in good deeds, which might allow the practitioner to accumulate good karma, but will never cause the cosmic light bulb to go on.

Instead, the rational mind must be tricked into letting its guard down long enough so that we can catch a glimpse of our Buddha nature. Thus the enigmatic and anti-logical questions known in Japanese as koans, the most famous of which is, "What is the sound of one hand clapping?" There's no correct answer to the question. Its purpose is to exhaust the rational mind into collapsing in a heap, clearing the way for moments of insight known as satori. Sometimes this is accomplished by physical means: a Zen master might whack his pupil with a stick or twist his nose. The goal, once again, is to transcend the fears and barriers erected by the conscious mind, leading us to recognize our own "surpassing self."

And despite Li's criticisms of Zen, much of what he says sounds very Zen-like. For example: "In genuine cultivation practice, one must cultivate one's own heart and inner self. One should search inside oneself rather than outside." This obviously contradicts his demands elsewhere that students show complete devotion to his writings.

Eliminating Karmic Debt

*F*inally, let's take a look at karma, the universal law of cause and effect that governs rebirth. A belief in it allowed the Chinese, during the disintegration of the Han dynasty, to understand the reason for their sufferings: they were paying for the sins of a past lifetime. But karma also offered hope that if, from now on, they were to lead morally correct lives, things would be better the next time around. Karma also allowed average citizens to bear more easily the haughty abuse of corrupt officials. They believed that, according to karmic law, these bureaucrats, although momentarily powerful and seemingly free from retribution, would receive their just desserts when they were reborn as pond scum.

Not for nothing, then, does Li incorporate karma as a key notion in Falun Gong. Today's Chinese also enjoy the prospect of tainted bureaucrats writhing in flames. Li explains that "a bad deed incurs a karmic debt." Unlike Buddhists, he doesn't use the phrase "bad karma," but simply "karma." But that's mere semantics. Bad deeds will come back to haunt you under both systems. Li lists these deeds in two categories: the serious (taking life) and the annoying (bullying others, scrambling for personal profits, and speaking ill of or acting unfriendly towards others).

But there's another difference between Buddhist karma and Li's equivalent. For the Buddha, karma is strictly a personal affair. The emphasis is on self-improvement; your karmic destiny isn't chained to that of your ancestors. Li, however, true to his mix-and-match philosophy, blends the Taoist idea of ch'eng-fu, or transmission of burden, into his basically Buddhist theory. Transmission of burden means that the sins of the fathers influence the destiny of their descendants — and Li teaches that ancestors may accumulate karma and pass it on as a legacy (either good or bad) to future generations.

How can we rid ourselves of accumulated karma — or, in Li's phrase, burn it off? Buddhism refuses to accept that everything that happens to us is due to actions committed in the past. As David J. Kalupahana explains, "The Buddha taught that karma is only one of the contributing factors in the evolution of the human personality. As important as having acquired merit in the past life is life in appropriate surroundings and proper resolve and application." Thus, the present tense counts for something, and even an evil-doer can guarantee a happy existence in the future by attempting to change his personality. Or, as the

Buddha put it, "Action is the field, consciousness the seed, and craving the moisture which leads to the rebirth of a being."

Li seems to accept that changes can be made to karmic debt in the present but, rather than focusing on positive action, insists that karma is burned off by cultivating xinxing and by undergoing "tribulations." As he puts it, "the tribulations and misfortunes you encounter in life are consequences of karma, for which you have to pay." Thus the attitude of those practitioners who have said they embrace the brutality of the police because it gives them the opportunity to get rid of, or chip away at, karmic debt and elevate their xinxing — their virtue or moral standing.

Li's teachings in this regard are dangerously close to the self-induced misery of the ascetic Jains, and are very un-Chinese. Historically, the Chinese have always been a trifle leery even of the Buddha's First Noble Truth. They weren't, and for the most part aren't, big fans of suffering. Rather, they are optimistic, and conceive of life as essentially good and well worth enjoying.

Other than these differences, however, Li is firmly in the Buddhist camp, and links karma to non-violence in an explicit way: "Taking life is the worst evil-doing crime and will accumulate heavy karmic debts . . . some 'qigong masters' even go hunting. Where is their mercy? Neither the Buddha school nor the Tao school acts against the Cosmic Law. Hunting is an act of killing."

At the same time, however, Li warns against the sort of obsessive, anti-karma paranoia displayed by the Jains, who could scarcely leave their houses for fear that they'd murder countless minute creatures and, in so doing, incur karmic debt. Instead, Li joins the Buddha in preaching the vital importance of context and intention. Karma is acquired if an action is malevolent, but if some unfortunate circumstance arises that's really nobody's fault, then no karma can be assigned to anyone. A degree of common sense is required, and (once again) Li cites the Buddha, who chided a disciple who fretted over whether to wipe out the bathtub, which was full of worms. The Buddha's reasonable request was that the disciple wipe it out. Li's point (and the Buddha's) is that it's all well and good to be moral and practise no-harming, but one shouldn't become paralyzed through over-zealous adherence to a moral code. "It is a kind of attachment," says Li, "if you live under constant fear of doing anything wrong." Rather, he adds, one should trust in a built-in safety mechanism: "Make light of your personal interests and be kind-hearted, and you will never commit wrong-doings because whatever you do is out of your compassion."

The Way to Nirvana

Let's review the basic building blocks of Li's teachings. His most quoted warning ("destroy the attachments") is lifted directly from the Buddha's Second and Third Noble Truths. His curative law bodies and his emphasis on longevity and physical health, along with the cosmic faluns he plants in practitioners' abdomens, are appropriations from Taoist Inner Alchemy, cross-referenced with basic qigong breathing techniques.

The concept of "emptiness" is Buddhist in origin, as is Li's insistence on the importance of causality, which is part and parcel of Dependent Origination. Yes, he places emphasis on his writings, and modifies the concept of karma by dragging in a person's ancestors to account for its accumulation. But even here, he may be making a bow in the direction of Taoism (ancestral karmic influence is a Taoist idea) and the Confucian (even Communistic) preoccupation with the importance of the collective.

All of which brings us almost to the end of a long and winding road — the attainment of Nirvana.

If a Buddhist has followed with diligence the Four Noble Truths and the Eight-Fold Path, he may achieve the cessation of craving, the root of all suffering, and achieve the *summum bonum* of enlightenment. But Li, true to form, adds an additional hurdle. Falun Gong teaches that to achieve enlightenment, one has to suffer "loss," which means "giving up such evil thoughts and immoral conducts as greed, gains, lust, desires, killing, fighting, stealing, robbing, fraudulence, and jealousy. If one wants to enter high-level cultivation, he also has to give up all inherent obsessions with desires, i.e. give up all his attachments."

The Dalai Lama describes the state of an enlightened Buddhist as follows: "He takes no delight in being shown respect. If he is slighted, he shows no anger. His wisdom is like an ocean. These are the hallmarks of the truly wise."

Li follows suit, by claiming that he himself qualifies for this exalted stratum. "No normal person can break my peace," he says. "I won't feel happy because someone has said something nice about me, nor will I get cross if someone should scold me . . . If you can let go of whatever you hold onto, you will certainly be able to keep your mind clear and clean."

But, as we will shortly demonstrate, Li does "get cross" when someone crosses him. Indeed, he gets positively apoplectic — ill befitting a person whose mind is spotless and transparent.

The Master Speaks

*M*any of Li's writings over the years provide ample evidence that there are at times, at least to the Western reader, spiritually distracted hands on the Falun Gong wheel. He has always been prone to remarks such as: "flying saucers of extra-terrestrials can travel back and forth at an inconceivable speed and become large or small. They have taken another alternative method of development, which is another scientific approach." Then there are his frequent references to Atlantis-like lost continents and cultures that lie perfectly preserved at the bottom of the sea. "Who created these civilizations tens of millions of years ago?" he inquires. "At that time, our human race was not even apes."

Besides his fondness for speaking in tongues (a "cosmic language of subtle beings in a space only a little bit higher than ours"), Li also likes the idea of aliens. At one point, he informed a reporter from *Time* magazine that "One type of alien looks like a human, but has a nose made of bone; others resemble ghosts." He went on to confide that the aliens had been around since the turn of this past century, and had not been idle: "Everyone believes that scientists invent things on their own, when in fact they are manipulated by aliens."

Aliens, Li went on to assert, already control the spirits and minds of any number of human beings. The reporter, bemused, asked Li if he was of this earth. Li replied that he didn't want to talk about himself at a higher level because nobody would understand him. In fairness, few of us haven't yearned to lead a reporter around by the nose. On the other hand, Li may not be kidding.

More serious are Li's claims, which stretch back to the early days of Falun Gong, that he is the sole possessor of cosmic truths. Sometimes he exercised a degree of control, as when he stipulated that "one should never use Buddhism to measure the Great Law of Zhen-Shan-Ren, because it is beyond measurement."

Sometimes he was more proprietary, noting that "The doctrines of the Great Law of Falun Dafa can give guidance to anyone in their cultivation, including those who have other religious beliefs. This is the Principle of the universe, the true Law that has never before been revealed. In the past humans were not allowed to know the Principle of the universe; it transcends all the sciences and moral principles of ordinary human society from ancient times to the present. What has been taught in religions and what people have experienced [to now] are only

Falun Gong practitioners
meditate in Tiananmen Square
before the crackdown.

TOP: The search for qi attracts
Easterners and Westerners alike.

BOTTOM: "Falun Dafa" spelled out by
practitioners in Australia, summer 1999.

TOP: Li speaks in Toronto, May 1999. Behind him, a poster portrays him as "the supreme Buddha."

BOTTOM: In spring 1999, Falun Gong practitioners — such as these devotees in Amsterdam — surface in many European cities.

TOP: The "holding-the-wheel-before-the-head" position is demonstrated outside of Toronto's City Hall, May 1999.

MIDDLE: While their fellow practitioners in China are persecuted, these Americans in Washington, DC, enjoy the freedom to meditate in public.

BOTTOM: Falun Gong teaches that enlightenment can be attained if one follows "three universal truths": Zhen (truth), Shan (benevolence), and Ren (endurance).

TOP: A mass demonstration of Falun Gong practitioners is held outside Toronto's City Hall, May 1999.

BOTTOM: Li Hongzhi is mobbed by his followers on a visit to Toronto, May 1999.

TOP: Thousands of practitioners demonstrate non-violently, assuming the "serene and peaceful countenance," Beijing, spring 1999.

MIDDLE: The crackdown: Chinese police violently haul Falun Gong members away from Tiananmen Square, as China prepares for its National Day celebrations, September 1999.
— CP PICTURE ARCHIVE, AP PHOTO/GREG BAKER

BOTTOM: On July 29, 1999, Chinese government bulldozers crush thousands of Falun Gong tapes on meditation and exercise. President Jiang Zemin had ordered the destruction of one and a half million books, and declared the Falun Gong illegal.
— CP PICTURE ARCHIVE, AP PHOTO/XINHUA

LEFT: Li Chang, Communist Party executive in the Chinese security forces, was sentenced to 18 years of hard labour for his role as a Falun Gong leader of the Beijing protests.

BELOW: Plain-clothed and uniformed police struggle with a practitioner during a protest in November 1999. — CP PICTURE ARCHIVE, AP PHOTO/STRINGER

Before retreating into silence,
Li Hongzhi visits Toronto, May 1999.

真　善　忍

ZHEN ~ *Truth*

SHAN ~ *Benevolence*

REN ~ *Endurance*

superficialities and phenomena, while its [Falun Dafa's] extensive and profound inner meaning can only present itself to and be felt and understood by the cultivators who are at different levels of their true cultivation, and they can really see what the Law is."

By December 1998, however, Li began to take his rhetoric up a couple of notches. Not content with exclusivity, he seemed to be constructing an enemies list, and relegated anyone who stood against him to the pit: "As for those with ulterior motives who dare to even slander Buddha Fa and Buddhas, they have already become ghosts in hell; it's just that their lives on earth are not over yet."

Lately, matters have become far worse. In June 2000, Li chose to address the topic of current events in China, and penned a quite remarkable outburst entitled "In Reference to a Prophecy." It begins by dragging in Nostradamus, and reads, in part, that Nostradamus's murky allusion to "the year 1999, seventh month," during which "from the sky will come a . . . Terror, in order to bring back to life the . . . king . . ." refers explicitly to the Central Committee of the Chinese Communist Party, which had used its power to initiate "a vicious, comprehensive suppression of Dafa and Dafa disciples."

Then, on July 16, 2000, Li surpassed himself. For well over a year, his followers had endured the most ghastly deprivations in his cause, while he, for the most part, had kept mum. Now, it was time to set the record straight.

This letter or epistle or whatever it is, is entitled "Towards Consummation," referring to the method of completing cultivation and departing the physical realm. Written in Li's customary baroque style, it upbraids what he perceives to be a lack of enthusiasm among his followers for his spiritual writings, and rails against a contaminated world and the dark forces that control it. Three other letters followed, all in a similar vein, but this example will more than suffice.

"Towards Consummation" begins with the usual reminder that "attachments" cause suffering, and that, "When a person enters this world, it is karmic arrangements that determine his course of life as well as what will be gained in it." So far, so good — this is old-time predestination.

Then come a number of recriminations directed at the backsliding faithful: "Are you continuing on the path because of those human attachments? If so, you cannot be counted as my disciple. Those who have been sifted out, during the evil-wrought tests that Dafa has encountered in China, are all people who have not relinquished those attachments." Here the trouble begins in earnest. What does "sifted out" mean? Is Li referring to those who were tortured and killed? Or is he speaking directly to those who weren't, because they didn't go out and demonstrate, those who lay low and never came forward or who stopped demonstrating, deciding not to risk their lives for a movement whose leader had retreated over the hills and far away?

Next, Li goes on to suggest that the police are in some strange way his agents, and that the privations endured by the practitioners are a necessary if not desirable ordeal. (This conclusion, as we have seen, had already been reached by some of his followers.) "Think about it, everyone!" he commands. "The enormous test at present is to see how Dafa fares and how students conduct themselves in Master's absence. How could Master speak out? How could I again tell you what to do?"

If by this statement he's admonishing practitioners for their inability to shed their attachments, he next appears to be blaming them for their persecution: "Were you truly able to discard those fundamental human attachments in your cultivation practice, these last trials and tribulations wouldn't have been so vicious." In other words, they brought it upon themselves.

Li seems to be upset by the dwindling attention span evidenced by practitioners who were being trucked off to torture and death: "Even now some people still can't concentrate on reading the books. When your mind is all over the place as you read, the countless Buddhas, Dao's, and Gods in the book see your laughable and pitiful mind, and can tell that the karma in your thoughts is controlling you, which is detestable."

After this comes even more bizarre sermonizing: "When I questioned the last group of high-level beings who are about to be eliminated why they have been concocting rumors about me and Dafa, they replied, 'There's no other way. The path you have taken is so righteous. How else could Dafa and your disciples be tested?'"

There doesn't seem to be much point in asking, but who are these mysterious beings who face elimination? Do they exist only in Li's fevered imagination, or do they bear some relation to reality?

Finally, the letter reaches its apocalyptic climax, with a swing at "Those vile human beings that have been used by sinister, old malicious forces." Fortunately, however, "The wicked and evil will soon be eliminated, the vile ones in the human world will receive due retribution, and sins will no longer be allowed to continue. Disciples are waiting to reach Consummation, and I can wait no more."

Nor, predictably, could Falun Gong practitioners, who rose to the challenge on July 20 by returning in force to Tiananmen Square. These demonstrations, which continued for a week, saw approximately two hundred protesters a day trucked off to a stadium in western Beijing. They apparently merited Li's commendation. He immediately posted a Web site message addressed to Falun Gong associations everywhere, but targeted specifically at true believers in mainland China. It explicitly condoned the latest round of protests, as follows: "It is definitely not wrong to explain the facts of our situation to the Chinese government in a peaceful manner. Over the past year, you have clarified the truth and appealed to people in the world and governments with a heart of kindness. You have done this in quite a righteous manner."

This was one of the very few times that Li had deigned to praise his followers — but along with praise came a far more typical admonition, warning them against undue zeal and stressing the need to address their higher duties: "I also hope that in the future, while clarifying the truth and appealing to the Chinese government, they will not in any way neglect the importance of studying the Fa, because all of them need to progress towards Consummation. I am paying close attention to everything the students are doing and the state of their cultivation. I hope that all of you handle things even better."

The Troubled Buddha

*M*ore recently, we have seen cult-like facets to Falun Dafa (although not to be mistaken with the likes of David Koresh or Jim Jones and, given the persecution of China, not unlike Christianity during the Roman persecutions). Gone now from Falun Gong's Web sites are photographs of the likeable man in a rumpled open shirt speaking casually and comfortably into the microphones before a huge audience in Canton during the summer of 1995, referring (despite his distaste for politics) to "those with the extreme leftist analysis of history."

Now, Li appears as an archetypal Buddha figure, posed atop the traditional lotus flower, thus signifying the enlightened man who floats above the muck of human weakness, just as the pristine bloom bobs gently on the surface of a brackish pond. He is customarily surrounded by a Buddhist mandala, is wrapped in a saffron robe, and wears a rather saccharine expression on his face.

He does not look in the least upset, but in fact, Li's anger has grown apace, as has his possessiveness. The Buddha argued that most human suffering is caused by identifying ourselves with what we are not. We say my wife, my husband, my new car, my profession, my country, my god. The price we pay for this ever-widening circle of ownership is fear, because the more things that we insist are ours, the more likely we are to feel pain, humiliation, and rage when we're disappointed or betrayed.

A Buddhist would instantly recognize Li Hongzhi as an angry and fearful man, a man whose followers are his chattels. He speaks of his practitioners, his disciples. They work for him, their Master. If he can't save them, no one else can. This ever-widening ownership encircles the globe, and so too does Li's fear and pain. All around him, he begins to detect real or imagined plots and betrayals. And when he wakes tomorrow in his secret hideaway, his rest will have been disturbed by troubled dreams.

Four

The Future of
Falun Gong

The year 1845 saw the beginning of the Taiping Rebellion. It was led by Hong Xiu Quan, who claimed to have had a dream in which he saw himself in the presence of God the Father, Mother Mary, and a middle-aged Jesus Christ. Hong therefore surmised himself to be God's Chinese son, Christ's Oriental brother. He also claimed that God had explicitly directed him to restore the true faith (that is, Christianity) to China by means of killing off the "demons and devils" — in other words, China's interloping Manchu overlords. Thus, not for the first time, a foreign religion promoted by a hallucination-prone zealot became an excuse to mobilize the Chinese to strike back against a hated government.

The ensuing uprising, which was centred in Nanjing, sliced the country in two. The bloodshed lasted until Hong's army was defeated in 1864. To put this struggle in context, the American Civil War was fought at about the same time, and accounted for approximately 365,000 deaths. The Taiping Rebellion cost

30 million lives, if one counts bodies both on the battlefields and in the ditches, dead as a result of famine and starvation.

Other examples might also be cited. Few people in the West have heard of the Yellow Turban and White Lotus rebellions, let alone Muslim uprisings in Yunan and Gansu. All were slaughters of epic proportions, ignited by religious upheaval, and supported (or carried out) by the peasantry. The Boxer Rebellion, which began in 1896, is better known, because it pitted the xenophobic Boxers against Christians, particularly the very few Westerners living in Beijing. It was put down only by means of punitive Western military expeditions. The Chinese Civil War itself, which the Communists won in large part because the peasants were on their side, left approximately 10 million dead. More recently, during the 1960s, Mao's Cultural Revolution was waged with all the fervour of a jihad, and claimed tens of thousands of lives.

In sum, the Chinese have always associated the emergence of a new religion, a new political movement, or indeed civil unrest of any magnitude, with threats to, and the potential over-turning of, the status quo. That is why China has traditionally responded to these events with fire and sword.

During the period from 1845 to 1949 — from the beginning of the Taiping Rebellion to the end of the Civil War — an estimated 50 to 55 million people perished as the direct or indirect result of rebellion, military conflict, and purges of every kind. Either figure far exceeds the total deaths in World Wars I and II. Taking the higher estimate, and working (for convenience) on the basis of one hundred years, China therefore averaged approximately 550,000 deaths per year; 45,800 deaths per month; 10,576 deaths per week; 1,510 deaths per day; 62 deaths per hour; and slightly more than one death per minute.

These figures are without parallel, and difficult for the Western mind to comprehend. But the Chinese understand them very well, being blessed — or cursed, depending on one's point of view — with long memories of a long and turbulent history. For most of that history, China has considered itself under siege, menaced on every side. Foreign faiths from Christianity to Islam (indeed, to Buddhism itself) were routinely imposed upon the Chinese people. All were at odds with the inherently Chinese belief in ancestor worship, Confucianism, or Taoism. All offered evidence that China could never for one moment relax its vigilance or falter in its resolve to keep the world at bay. This is not paranoia, but fact. The Chinese have excellent reason to be wary of foreign incursion. They've always thought that someone was out to get them, and they were usually right. Calamity has always lurked, ready to challenge and perhaps topple the rulers of the day.

As we have seen, an early ruler would seek to confirm his legitimacy by responding decisively to these perils as they arose. This useful precedent drove Jiang Zemin to launch his suppression of Falun Gong, on the theory that the late twentieth century was a logical extension of what had gone before. If so, the Communist Party can plausibly be considered as just another dynasty.

What is its legitimacy? Its former foes (the Nationalist forces) were not entirely defeated. Instead, they sit mockingly in Taiwan, stocking up on American arms. The Party seems to be incapable of governing prudently and benevolently; it's riddled with corruption from top to bottom. It has parachuted in yet another alien system — Red Capitalism — and embarked on a crash program of re-tooling smokestack industries, eliminating state-run companies, and axing subsidies of every kind. This has resulted in rampant and unprecedented unemployment.

Hundreds of millions of Chinese find themselves disenfranchised and dispossessed. Peasants have been run off their co-operatives and their land, and have no way of making a living.

Social ills such as prostitution, AIDS, and drug use are skyrocketing. Crime, including extortion, is also rampant. Racial and linguistic minorities are under attack. All the traditional cracks and fissures are reappearing, but on a larger scale, and with even more frightening speed. This, if history is anything to go by, makes Jiang's regime — and the Party itself — prime candidates for decline and fall. The people are justifiably aggrieved, and have a right to remove them. But the people do not, as yet, have the means to do so.

That is why Jiang's regime has chosen to target Falun Gong. It explains the hysterical reaction of the Chinese government to entirely non-violent protesters who march daily into Tiananmen Square bearing portraits of an absent guru. The suppression of Falun Gong has virtually nothing to do with Falun Gong per se. No one seriously believes that its practitioners, especially without Li at the helm, constitute a revolutionary movement. They cannot supplant the Communist Party or remove a single Party official from power. They, in themselves, are utterly powerless.

But, if history is anything to go by, the appearance of new religious and spiritual movements have always been harbingers of social and political upheaval. They're lightning rods, barometers of impending change. Falun Gong is a straw in the gathering wind that might, given the right combination of circumstances, sweep the Communists aside — a symptom of a discontent so widespread and broadly based that it could boil over into actual rebellion. Falun Gong both portends what may come and echoes what has gone before. It is part of a recognized pattern that culminates in the defeat of an uncaring dynasty or regime.

Thus Jiang's responses to Falun Gong practitioners, and to Li. They are his primary targets, but they are not alone. China commits all manner of human rights violations daily — witness the measures taken against Tibetan Buddhists, Chinese Christians and Muslims, pro-democracy activists, parents who unwisely bear more than one child, and anyone who dares for whatever reason to deviate from that week's Party line. A list of all of China's atrocities would be wearisome indeed but, presented with such a list, the Chinese authorities wouldn't blink an eye. Not once have they denied their activities; not once have they bothered to excuse or apologize for them. These are strictly internal matters, China's own affairs.

But as Li Hongzhi sits who knows where in the United States, chatting away in cyberspace, the one inescapable fact is that he's not in China. This increases the Chinese government's paranoia. They don't know what he's up to, but they believe him to be in some way, shape, or form under American protection and influence. Thus, they conclude that Li himself has become a form of foreign intervention — if not an agent, then a puppet, of the West. Perhaps the U.S. is telling him what to say, or when to say it. There must be a hidden agenda buried amidst his Web site musings.

Is China altogether wrong in this conclusion? A list of America's meddlings around the world would be every bit as wearisome as an accounting of Chinese brutalities. Think of the installation of the Shah of Iran; the propping up of tinpot South American dictators; wars in Korea and Vietnam. Think also of how American intelligence agencies conducted what amounted to a covert war in Tibet, using Tibetan Buddhists as pawns (actions that were denounced by the Dalai Lama), and how these same agencies helped to ensure that various Christian movements would be instrumental in bringing down the Communist regimes in Poland and other parts of the former Soviet Empire, thus igniting (or so it was hoped) a power struggle within the Russian Communist Party. All these and more historical precedents conspire to give the Chinese leaders restless nights.

But these same leaders cannot pull the blankets over their heads and go back to sleep — or, more precisely, back to splendid Oriental isolation. When China embarked on its first tentative reforms in the 1980s under Deng Xiaoping, it set in motion a train of events that neither it nor the West could wholly control. China is no longer a closed system; it must deal with life beyond the Great Wall. Turning inward once again is not an acceptable option.

At the moment, China is mounting strenuous attempts to join the world community, and notably the World Trade Organization. It has no choice but to do so, and its leaders have already demonstrated that they fully understand what they are getting into. It's not hybrid Red Capitalism, but capitalism red in tooth and claw, a predatory arena in which the Chinese are already doing quite well: The Chinese enjoy a trade surplus of $42 billion U.S. with the world. But even harsher, more disruptive realities will presently be thrust upon them, and it will be interesting to see how they respond in the longer term.

The short-term questions are: What shape will China be in by the time the WTO rubber-stamps its application? Will it continue its trajectory as a relatively cohesive nation and emerging superpower? Or will it overreach itself and fall from grace as quickly as did the Soviet Union? What impact will it have on the world stage; what role will it play in shaping the directions of future international policies? Some observers have argued that the United States and other fully developed Western nations would like to see that role curtailed, at least for a while. It would suit their purposes if China came inside the WTO tent, but with begging bowl in hand, as a down-at-the-heels supplicant, weaker and more destabilized than its betters.

All this remains to be seen. The point is that China's relative strengths and weaknesses will do much to determine its perceptions of the real or imagined threats it will face from all points of the compass — and, in particular, its future responses to Falun Gong.

The Resurgence of Religion

*C*ontemporary China is a country in the grip of ideological chaos and unprecedented change. Over the course of the past fifty years, it has functioned as a sort of human laboratory, devoid of all ethical restraints. First, the Chinese were wrenched from a largely feudal society into the aggressive social experiment that was Maoist collectivization and thought reform. Next, Mao went into the ideological dustbin, and China was thrown into the deep end of the modern, post-industrialized world.

Within the span of two generations, China's social rituals and belief systems have been turned on their heads three times. The death of millions by starvation in the economic disaster of the Great Leap Forward and the violent, senseless purges of the Cultural Revolution, coupled with economic stagnation, political corruption, and unceasing atrocity climaxing in the 1989 massacre in Tiananmen Square, have destroyed what little faith the Chinese people ever had in their country's particular relationship with Communism. Under such circumstances, everyone needs something to believe in. Without a psychological footing, the Chinese turned in any number of directions — to Christianity, to other faiths, and to Falun Gong.

"All traditional cultures," writes Robert Lifton, "have provided opportunities for, and made space for, the experience of transcendence, but in the postmodern world such opportunities seem diminished or marginalized. The hunger for them, however, remains, and becomes bound up with our myriad confusions."

This hunger for transcendence found one postmodern expression in the plethora of New Age movements that recently swept the United States. But it exists also, and even more keenly, in China, which many people would consider a traditional culture. That's true, but only to a degree. China's traditions, as we have seen, have been interrupted by the state. Its changes have been so recent and so violent that there's been no tranquil space, no opportunity for the Chinese to pause and reflect, to draw breath and decide what they need and want.

Of course, even if they did decide, it wouldn't do them any good. A roller-coaster ride of conflicting ideologies has been imposed upon them. There is little wonder that the role of the individual in Chinese society is unclear: People no longer have any idea what may be expected or demanded of them during a given week.

Thus the current resurgence of religion in all its forms that has re-entered China's collective national consciousness at its time of greatest need. The age-old and deeply curative ideas of Confucianism, Taoism, and Buddhism, whose profound resonance was never lost despite half a century's chaos, have returned in the guise of other doctrines — specifically, Falun Gong.

Li Hongzhi's appearance on the scene coincided with a time of intense political cynicism, continuing confusion, and a general disinclination to embrace wholeheartedly Red Capitalism, the latest official panacea. All of this paved the way for his message, which at the outset at least was real and positive — thus its instant and widespread acceptance. He was indeed, as his brother Donghui told us, the right man in the right place at the right time, armed with the right stuff. He stressed compassion for one's fellows and warned that an attachment for material things brings only temporary happiness, obscuring the greater needs of the human heart. He also did his practitioners demonstrable good. If you didn't buy into his murky prose and wilder flights of fancy, you could still benefit from Falun Gong's physical exercise regime.

In his wholesale borrowings from Taoism, Confucianism, and especially Buddhism, Li offered his followers a simple and much-longed-for moral code. He counselled tolerance and understanding, even of one's enemies. He taught simplicity in life, constant self-examination, and personal discipline through meditation. All these teachings were tempered by a practical understanding and acceptance of the world. Governments were to be respected; business was an honourable enterprise. Li never demanded that his followers turn their backs on society, abandoning it as corrupt and vile. Instead, he exhorted them to pursue their chosen professions to the best of their abilities and to enjoy the fruits of their labours, as long as they behaved fairly and kept a sense of perspective.

To this non-radical and non-subversive message, Li added icing on the cake. Through his adaptation of qigong exercises and established breathing techniques, he encouraged practitioners to lead lives that were not only mentally healthy but physically robust. Strip away the more far-fetched aspects of his system (law bodies and aliens), and it's no surprise that millions of Chinese should have chosen to follow Li's banner.

For them, Li effectively filled a spiritual vacuum in their society, but his role was in fact deeper, more complex, and multifaceted. Decades of cynical power grabs and political corruption, coupled with Jiang Zemin's lack of charisma, had left the Chinese without an emperor — or at least, an emperor with a visible suit of clothes. That is why Li was instantly recognized as a strongman, a familiar figure in Chinese history. For millions, he became — with what to us seems mind-boggling speed — "the Teacher," "the Master," a paternal figure who enjoyed as well the advantage of novelty, a fresh sole possessor of cosmic truths.

So powerful were the effects of Li's message and physical presence that his fame was not appreciably lessened when he fled the country, leaving his followers to fend for themselves. Now, almost two years of arrests, torture, and murder have failed to destroy (or even, it seems, dampen) their commitment; and the government, grudgingly, has had to admit the tremendous resilience of Falun Gong.

Master Li and the West

*A*ll of which raises several vital questions. What awaits Li and Falun Gong in China, and on the world stage? Can he hope to enjoy similar success in North America and Europe? Are Li's fate and the fate of Falun Gong inextricably linked? That is, could it survive, in China or elsewhere, without him, if he abandoned it or it abandoned him? Would Falun Gong disintegrate, or has the last year of ceaseless struggle proven that the movement has outgrown its creator?

First, let's look at Li's chances in North America and throughout the world. His desire for expansion, particularly within the United States, is obvious. To qualify as a world religion (or spiritual movement, or whatever you choose to call it), Falun Gong will have to attract hundreds of thousands of new practitioners. It has failed to do so, for a variety of reasons. It's making gradual inroads into the West, spurred by Web sites from Moscow to Sydney, Australia, that translate Li's daily insights (including turgid poetry) into every language imaginable. Anyone with a computer can download his training cassettes. But Falun Gong's popularity abroad is overwhelmingly concentrated in Chinese expatriate communities in Canada and the United States, where he is deeply revered. To take Falun Gong to another level, new converts will have to come from outside the Chinese diaspora.

The huge discrepancy between Li's success in China and his relative lack of it so far in the West is easily explained. First, in the West, Falun Gong is not the powerful political symbol it is in China, where it forms the only opposition to the Communist Party and the most serious threat to Party hegemony in fifty years. As well, what success has indeed been achieved beyond China's borders has been in spite of, not because of, Li. The more one learns about his latest digressions, not to mention his seeming abandonment of his flock, the less attractive a figure he becomes in Western eyes. The West is already in what might be described as an era of post–New Age spirituality, having seen all manner of gurus strut and fret away their hour on the stage, with the result that peculiar, mystical beliefs are greeted with far more skepticism than they were ten years ago.

But disinclination to climb aboard the Falun Gong band-wagon does not equal outright condemnation. On the contrary, throughout the United States and Canada, hundreds of cities have seen fit to designate an official Falun Gong (or Falun Dafa) Day — and, in some cases, a Week. Numerous honorary citizen-ships have been conferred, in absentia, on Li. We highly doubt that the civic officials who read these pronouncements have taken the trouble to read Li's books, or know anything much about Falun Gong. Rather, these recognitions have come about because of extremely able lobbying activities on the part of Falun Gong groups, who are keen to counteract Communist propa-ganda, while at the same time acquiring instant (if relatively superficial) credibility and exposure in the West.

Falun Gong's Web sites happily list, on an almost daily basis, the latest town or city, no matter how small, that's been moved to acknowledge Falun Gong's struggle — but many such centres, to be frank, do not appear to be hotbeds of spiritual awareness. They include Fayetteville, Arkansas (population 62,000); Port Moody, British Columbia (population 20,000); Deerfield Beach, Florida (population 50,000); and League City, Texas (popula-tion 52,000).

Heartening as these gestures may be, they indicate a purely token political acceptance — vicarious admiration, not ideolog-ical or spiritual endorsement. Thanks to the heroic sacrifices of its practitioners, Falun Gong has come to be synonymous with Chinese human rights abuses to such a degree that Tibetan Buddhists and Chinese Christians are getting lost in the shuffle.

The squeaky wheel gets the media attention — and, to put it bluntly, the knee-jerk liberal reaction.

For the towns and cities involved, the declaration of a Falun Gong Day is a mixture of genuine sympathy for, and admiration of, a group that's plainly suffered much, a chance to get behind a motherhood issue at zero risk, a final parting shot at Communism (now that Russia's Evil Empire is being run by the Mafia), and a sop to voters of Chinese extraction. It has not and will not draw fresh converts to the Falun Gong fold.

How, then, can Li hope to broaden his base? It's no use to maintain, as do Li's adherents, that until one actually practises Falun Gong one doesn't have the right to form an opinion. In reality, a person who's vaguely interested in learning more about Li's teachings is apt to locate a copy of *China Falun Gong*, or visit one of the group's many Web sites. (The Minghui, or "all-seeing celestial wisdom," site appears to be operated by Li's core group of American apostles, and offers an unusually vibrant experience.)

As we've indicated, some of Li's teachings are valuable and good. In them, sophisticated Westerners will recognize his take on concepts found in many other Eastern spiritual traditions. But a chance encounter with Falun Gong is not an easy prospect. Li's writings and other communications are at times inaccessible, off-putting, obscure, old hat, and often difficult to take seriously. His self-aggrandizement wears uneasily, and his inability to differentiate between science and fantasy places him dangerously close to dismissal.

He seems unwilling to put any effort into making Falun Gong more responsive to Western needs. Instead, the West is supposed to respond to Falun Gong in its raw, unadapted form. Unfortunately, just for openers, the West doesn't believe in Atlantis. Potential practitioners are bound to ask themselves how, if Li is willing to talk in so cavalier a fashion about science, he can be entrusted with real people's hearts and souls. No less an authority than the Dalai Lama has said on various occasions, with perhaps a sigh of rueful resignation, that "when science points to or proves a truth contrary to Buddhist teaching, then Buddhist teaching must change."

This remark brings us to yet another strike against Li's ability to make inroads into the West. Unfortunately for him, Buddhism got there first. Witness Whittier, California, a town originally founded by Quakers, where former president Richard Nixon went to college. But Whittier is also home to the $30-million Hsi Lai Temple, which made news last year by donating $55,000 to Al Gore's presidential campaign. Completed in 1988, it is today the largest Buddhist monastery in the United States, a symbol of the emergence (indeed, the entrenchment) of Buddhism in the American religious, social, and political landscape.

Li's ongoing fascination with Buddhism is obvious; it's the reason he protests too much. In fact, he'd like to be on the Buddha's lily pad, because — with 350 million adherents worldwide — Buddhism is the world's fifth largest religion. In the United States, it's no longer considered an "alternative" spiritual path, but a mainstream faith. Few people would fail to admit its basic legitimacy, or dream of referring to it as a cult. In 1960, a generous estimate of the number of practising American Buddhists would have been somewhere around 200,000. Today, there are 3 million, a more than ten-fold increase in only forty years.

How has Buddhism managed to strike such a responsive chord? To discover the answer, we need only contrast it with some of Li's more doubtful activities. While Li adopts a confrontational position, characterizing the West as hopelessly corrupt, Western Buddhists have learned to be more optimistic, more outreaching. In short, Buddhism has shed much of its more esoteric baggage to concentrate instead on the very tangible value of the Buddha's psychological approach.

As a result, Westerners who find themselves drawn to Eastern wisdom are far more likely to investigate the traditional, rather than an eclectic, sometimes seemingly fantastical hybrid. Westerners want to be met half way, and Buddhism often does. This willingness is expressed by Lama Surya Das, who writes in an article featured on the American Buddhist Center Web site entitled "Ten Emerging Trends of Western Dharma" that "the Dharma is very suited to the Western way of life. It need not be complicated, mysterious, or fancy. Buddha Dharma is ordinary life, including everything from meditation to relationship yoga and parenting practice. Among other things, it involves itself with the body-mind connection, which might well include suggestions like eating right, exercising right, and having a sense of humour."

Lama Das is only one of a large number of articulate voices raised on Buddhism's behalf. Westerners have paid attention over the years to writers such as Alan Watts, and figures such as the Dalai Lama, who in the 1950s and 1960s would travel from his exile in India to California, France, Germany, and England to speak about the healing powers of the dharma. His seemly behaviour won many friends, and led to a great many high-profile converts — no guarantee of legitimacy or superiority, nor a sure-fire yardstick of success, but very useful when it comes to garnering favourable publicity. Falun Gong has not developed in this regard. Li has no second-in-command, and Falun Gong has no visible spokespersons.

While Li finds fascination in Nostradamus, Western Buddhism is busy casting off a whole lot of exotic ballast. As Chogyam Trungpa puts it in *The Myth of Freedom and the Way of Meditation*: "The bodhisattva's discipline is to relate to earth properly, to relate to his sense and mind properly . . . ignoring earth to chase after psychic phenomena is like the play of children trying to find gold at the end of the rainbow. We do not concern ourselves with the cosmic world, the world of gods, psychic powers, angels and devils. To do so may be to lose track of the physical world in which we live, and this results in madness."

Lama Das welcomes the shedding of "complex, esoteric rites and arcane rituals. Western teachers stress essence more than form, as well as teachings that are tolerant for daily life. It is thus practical and this-world oriented, rather than otherworldly and hermetic, with great emphasis on integrating Dharma practice via mindfulness and compassion into daily life."

Perhaps the problem (for Li and Falun Gong) is that Buddhism, having been around for a while, has had the opportunity to plant roots in the West, gain a feel for the territory, develop a track record, and tailor its message to a different audience. Li has not yet done any of these things.

Whether he likes it or not, Li must reckon with the great American melting pot. But his every action — seclusion, petulance, woolly thinking, outrageous claims, and gathering paranoia — militates against success. If Falun Gong is to survive and prosper in the West, Li would do well to tear a page from the Buddhist book, or risk relegation to the spiritual backwoods.

Let the final word go to Lama Das, who observes that "most Westerners seem to have a true appreciation for many different meditation techniques and traditions. We have seen how politics, the quest for power, and sectarian bias have created chaos within various religious communities. We understand it is essential that we strive diligently not to fall into those same traps. As practitioners, we are generally interested in broadening and deepening our experience of the various Buddhist spiritual practices. I think it is safe to say that there is a true appreciation of the benefits of non-sectarianism, ecumenism, and cross-fertilization. In fact, many teachers are already synthesizing the best of the various traditions into one amalgamated Western Dharma that seems inevitable. American karma is our great melting pot. We have to live with that and make the most of it."

Falun Gong's Uncertain Future

*I*n the summer of 2000, the prognosis for Falun Gong's survival in China, let alone its prosperity, did not look at all promising. Li's adherents were losing badly in the war of attrition inflicted upon them by President Jiang's security apparatus. The disciples soldiered on without Li, and practitioners in North America and abroad attempted to maintain an international presence without him at the helm.

By this time, Li's withdrawal was seen as a huge strategic blunder, a self-inflicted blow against Falun Gong. To be a leader in exile is one thing; the Dalai Lama plays this role to the hilt. Li, however, had become a leader in hiding. No valid reason could be put forward for his silence, and there is no doubt that American and European political leaders viewed it with a jaundiced eye.

Li's own Web-site explanation — that sooner or later his flock would have to learn to get along without him — offered cold comfort. As the World Trade Organization continued its deliberations in Geneva and Washington, his absence made it easier for them to drop any thought of positing Falun Gong as a deal-breaking human rights issue that could block China's entry. (Although, to be fair, the Western leaders' collective amnesia was also induced by China's capitulation on other fronts — as when it jumped the human rights hurdle with a single bound by giving the West more than it had dreamed of receiving, principally entry into China's banking and telecommunications industries.)

In effect, Li appears for the moment to have marginalized

himself by failing to capitalize on the Western media's sympathy towards the plight of his followers in China. He didn't follow up or press his case, and thus squandered his moral capital and ensured that any stories of brutal repreession that did emerge from China continued to be one-dimensional and superficial, because Li wasn't available to provide context or background.

Then, when he finally broke his silence, his first postings on the Minghui Web site, as we've described, could hardly be considered illuminating, let alone inspirational. Given Li's chronic non-appearance, and his quirkiness when he chose to break his silence, the press verdicts grew more lukewarm. Perhaps Falun Gong was just another sect, which had captured the world's attention for a fleeting moment, but was now about to be ground into dust by the juggernaut of the Communist government's unabated persecution.

This view of Falun Gong was altered by the fresh round of demonstrations that followed Li's messages in late July 2000, which at least had the effect of forcing China's government, through the Communist Party–owned *People's Daily*, to admit that, despite a year of constant repression, it had been unable to crush Falun Gong. The article complained that "the cult will not voluntarily step down from the historical stage," thus compelling the Chinese authorities to gird themselves for a "long-lasting, complicated and acute struggle," and to recognize the need to crack down on Li's followers with a "firm hand."

This admission was quite remarkable, since it granted that Falun Gong's practitioners — ordinary Chinese men, women, and quite often children — had succeeded in mounting for an entire year a public and continuous opposition to the country's rulers. This was something that no other group had managed to accomplish in more than half a century. Worse yet, as far as the Chinese government was concerned, Li's followers showed few signs of abandoning the struggle or fading quietly away.

These facts provide a partial answer to one of our questions. Yes, Chinese Falun Gong practitioners have offered ample evidence that they can endure over the short term — if a number of crucial factors remain unchanged. But there is no guarantee that these factors *will* remain unchanged.

In order to fathom the short- to medium-term future of Falun Gong, we must examine a number of different scenarios. All involve in some measure the Chinese government, the practitioners, and Li Hongzhi himself.

Under the first scenario, things will continue pretty much as before. The practitioners will appear daily in Tiananmen Square, and will be dragged away. They will reiterate their perpetual request: that the government leave them alone to practise Falun Gong. This request will not be granted, because the government cannot lose face by admitting it was wrong. Fear drives the Communist regime, and dissent invites a deluge of woe, as does a show of weakness. If the authorities accommodate Falun Gong, then Tibetan Buddhists, Mongolian Muslims, pro-democracy activists, ethnic separatists, and everybody else under the sun will sit up, take notice, and decide to test the outside of the envelope. (In fact, this process has already begun. In October 2000, an exiled poet named Huang Beiling called explicitly on Chinese intellectuals to emulate Falun Gong's techniques, and embark on a program of civil disobedience.)

The Communist Party is unwilling to surrender one iota of political power to what they see as a bunch of troublemakers led by an offshore guru. The protesters may have only one string to their bow, but the government has run out of ideas as well. Their actions are morally bankrupt. They're also ineffectual. To act on the premise that you can subdue people by hauling them off to jail and torturing them is not a winning formula. It didn't work for Nero, who thought he could buy a bit of peace and quiet by feeding the early Christians to the lions, and it won't work for Jiang Zemin — but it's all he can think of. Thus, while the struggle envisioned by the *People's Daily* writer may indeed be "long-lasting" and "acute," it will not be "complicated." Sadly, it will probably be more and more of the same.

Of course, it could also be argued that Falun Gong's tactics, while morally upright, are also ineffectual. A year of protest has yielded no results, except broken bones and dozens of dead bodies. It's spiritual trench warfare — neither side is willing to give an inch. Indeed, it could be argued that the Falun Gong practitioners have formed an "attachment" for protest, an ennobling act that allows them to burn off karma and polish their xinxing. Taking that thought a step further, maybe they've formed an attachment for Li, who keeps sending them into the fray, and who has long since seemed to have run out of more useful strategies.

No matter. The point is that, for the next little while, the same dynamic is apt to keep playing over and over again, differing only in the operative level of official hypocrisy. This supposition is bolstered by the fact that, in September 2000, the Chinese government simultaneously launched a $7-million U.S. public-relations campaign to burnish its image prior to the Senate's vote on its trade status and an even more intensive round of religious persecution. As Oriental orchestras and troupes of acrobats wended their way across America, delighting the crowds in ten major cities, the police were working overtime at Tiananmen Square. (Of course, the United States is no stranger to this sort of double-think, having proclaimed itself the light of liberty while trying to bomb North Vietnam back into the Stone Age.)

So much for a continuation of the status quo. The next scenario involves a strategic withdrawal, a backing-off from the barricades.

This, for Falun Gong, may be a matter of necessity. The Communist Party's war of attrition may sap the practitioners' resolve, and thin out their numbers past the breaking point. They may find or feel themselves unable to maintain the current level of confrontation in the face of the government's unyielding response. In other words, even with 100 million true believers to call upon, Falun Gong may run out of martyrs.

We use this word advisedly; the willingness to suffer and, if necessary, die for one's beliefs has always been an essential part of any emerging movement, either religious or political. (Some would argue that the two are inseparable.) Such movements' credibility hinges on the number of people who are prepared to go to the wall, and Falun Gong's practitioners — strange as it sounds at this point in our narrative — have not responded en masse. Granting the existence of those 100 million true believers, the fact that only 10,000 demonstrators have ever engaged in overt protest at the same place and time leads us to the conclusion that the vast majority (including the many sympathizers and closet practitioners who remain in the Communist Party and the bureaucracy) have no wish to storm the barricades. They are biding their time in private — an entirely reasonable course of action, since there's no requirement in Li's teachings (as opposed to his Web site wanderings) that they rush out into public squares. Thus, we can see a period during which Falun Gong goes underground, which, for the most part, it has already done.

The next scenario hinges on the passage of time. Jiang is in his seventies — and, under the Chinese constitution (a flexible document, as we have seen), must step down in 2003. The

Communist regime may bend, but does not look like it will soon break, or be pushed aside.

Much is happening as you read these speculations, and the changes evident on Beijing's streets these days would have been unthinkable only a few short years ago. Ten minutes from Tiananmen Square, where Mao's gigantic portrait keeps rather abstract watch, thousands of young Chinese cavort in an ear-splitting discotheque, whose owners project archival footage of the Cultural Revolution onto television screens as a backdrop to a wild Saturday night.

If Li Hongzhi were to return tomorrow, he'd find himself a stranger in a strange land — one that might not be as receptive to his message as it was in the early 1990s. Now, billions of dollars in foreign investment flow daily into the country, as the population is urged to embrace the free market, becoming — as if by some alchemical process — instant entrepreneurs. The young and computer-literate may succeed in making the adjustment. Their elders, struggling to conform with the new, ever-shifting order, are utterly alone.

This process will continue, sped by China's presumed entry into the WTO. More rapidly than it hopes, China will be opened to the West, and subjected to new external pressures, new internal strife. It's not inconceivable that Jiang's successors will be astute enough to realize that, in that case, neither neo-Communist nor Red Capitalist dogma will suffice to hold the nation together.

Enter Falun Gong, which under this scenario would have several things going for it. First, a fair number of Party members would still be practitioners. Second, many of its teachings are tailor-made for a society that's undergoing future shock. Its practices and philosophical bases could only lead to social, political, and economic cohesion during a time of accelerated change, because Falun Gong teaches that forbearance requires its members to suffer tribulations gladly, converting karma into de, and so on.

Tomorrow's China is in for tribulations aplenty, and an upright group of practitioners could only provide a moral anchor. Thus, the prodigal demonstrators would be returned to acceptability — literally so, since they suffered no deprivations in the early 1990s. Hypothetically, Falun Gong could prove to be a tremendous asset to the Chinese state. It would require all sorts of political gymnastics, but it could be done. Everything would happen behind the scenes, because no Chinese regime is prepared to admit that it, or its immediate predecessor, was wrong. All that's required is a bit of breathing space.

Unfortunately, this bright scenario founders on none other than Li Hongzhi. No doubt the American intelligence community yearns for and anticipates the collapse of the current Communist regime, and may have believed that it had under its protection the leader of a Chinese state religion in waiting. But let us take a moment and see where these possibilities lead.

First, it's fair to say that President Jiang would like to see Li's head on a pole, so it's unlikely that Li will be getting on a flight to Beijing next week. But it's also fair to say that Jiang's as yet unknown successors may bridle at the prospect of Li's return — if, as would surely be the case, he would immediately embark on a victory tour, addressing stadiums full of rapturous followers. Yet even the Chinese government would have difficulty saying to 100 million practitioners something along the lines of: "All is forgiven, but not your fearless leader, who cannot come home again." Of course, Li may have absolutely no wish to do so. Perhaps he's perfectly happy to remain in the United States, where all seems — for the moment at least — "empty and full of light."

But, as history demonstrates, the best-laid plans of quasi-religious leaders can often go off the rails. Li might become embroiled in a scandal or be otherwise disgraced. He might be assassinated while out for a morning stroll. If any of the Communist government's more serious charges against him can be proved, that might be enough to spur the United States to view him as a liability, and put him more or less forcibly on the next plane to Beijing.

It's also possible that Li might go overboard, succumbing to full-blown megalomania, a condition defined by the *Psychiatric Dictionary* as someone's belief that he's possessed of greatness. Indeed, he may believe himself to be Christ, God, Napoleon, and — on good days — "everybody and everything." Already Li shows signs of doing so. It's hard to remain enthusiastic about a doctrine that preaches humility while its author claims that "At present, I am the only person in the world teaching orthodox Fa in public. I have done something unprecedented. I have further-more opened this door so widely in the Dharma-ending time [a period of general moral decline]. In fact, this opportunity does not come along in one thousand years or ten thousand years." Elsewhere, Li says that his teachings are "creating a new humankind," and adds that he can protect his disciples from death.

Li's claim to be the world's saviour clearly satisfies the definition of megalomania. Just as clearly, his inordinate fondness for implanting wheels and law bodies into his followers' mortal frames comes close to the idea that he's "everybody and every-thing." All these non-existent entities are part of his vision of himself, but raise the distinct possibility that, if he feels the constant need to convince himself and others that he is everything, he may be plagued by the terror that in fact he is nothing at all.

This would be in keeping with speculation on the probable mindset of a man who came from nowhere — who recognized himself as somehow different and potentially extraordinary. What, after all, was Li? An anonymous clerk with no familial or political contacts whatsoever, and therefore no hope of achieving conventional success. Like ninety-nine percent of the Chinese population, he was on the outside looking in. But through his creation of Falun Gong, he could grant his imagination full rein, appropriating unto himself the roles of society's most honoured and influential figures. As a spiritual leader of a large group of people, he would automatically be seen as both a holy man and a politician. As a self-described healer, he challenged medical doctors on their own turf.

What if Jiang's (or a subsequent) government winds up, for whatever combination of reasons, in deep trouble, unable to cope with change of abnormal magnitude? Falun Gong's practitioners are still on the loose, parading daily through Tiananmen Square. The government, tired of seeing them bounce back from detention after detention, might decide to crush them once and for all, lest they inspire even more widespread civil disobedience in response to greater woes.

The present regime, for all its excesses, has yet to officially impose the death penalty for the crime of being a Falun Gong member. Under certain circumstances, it might, and it just might start with the members of an "evil cult" that poses an ever more clear and present danger to an embattled state.

We put this very possibility to a number of North American practitioners, who dismissed it out of hand, saying that any government would be bound to capitulate before it engaged in such atrocities. But they went on to add that, if executions should in fact occur, the blame would lie squarely and solely with the government involved, because of its corruption, incompetence, and immorality.

Safe in North America, these practitioners are at risk of forgetting their own history. When push comes to shove, China will not be shoved. If its back is to the wall, the results might make us recall the bloodthirsty purges of the Cultural Revolution with fond nostalgia. All bets would at once be off, and Falun Gong would become the first, but not the last, scapegoat.

How the West would respond is almost too dire to contemplate. If, for whatever combination of reasons, Chinese social, political, and economic unrest seemed likely to topple a government, if China collapsed as did the former Soviet Union (a superpower that overnight found itself in ruin), or if it decided to launch a military attack on Taiwan, the fat would be in the fire — especially if the Chinese believed, rightly or wrongly, that the West had colluded in instigating any of the above.

Falun Gong practitioners would be unlikely to be among the last groups standing after such a cataclysm. Millions of people would be set in motion, and would no doubt meet with the same response that greeted the arrival on North American shores of a few hundred Chinese who attempted to flee the country in derelict boats. Upon landing, they must have felt right at home, since they were whisked away to detention centres.

On that apocalyptic note, we reluctantly leave our What If's behind, and return to the present tense. Like everyone else, we find the struggle between Falun Gong practitioners and President Jiang's regime a fascinating conflict, one that defies ordinary definitions and ready parallels. It is not, for example, a Gandhi-like clash of cultures. Gandhi turned to massive non-violent civil disobedience campaigns in order to expel the British colonialists and realize India's political independence. Falun Gong's techniques appear to be outwardly similar, but the two situations are in fact quite different. Obviously, the protesters aren't attempting to drive anyone out — instead, the battle rages within the confines of Chinese culture, religion, and race. And, despite what Li Hongzhi claims, it is a very political struggle.

Li may or may not have a political agenda, or political

ambitions of his own. We do know that his admonitions to shun politics are either hypocritical or naive, because he keeps an essentially political pressure on the Chinese government through the actions of his followers. Gandhi was forthright, remarking that, "He who says there are no politics in religion doesn't understand religion."

It is doubly naive for Falun Gong's practitioners to claim that all they want is to be left alone, free not only from persecution on the part of the Chinese regime, but of interference of any kind from any other quarter.

By refusing to define either himself or Falun Gong politically, Li has allowed Jiang to do it for him. Jiang and his cohorts have seized the opportunity with both hands, not because they're defending anything as lofty (or bankrupt, whichever you prefer) as Communist ideology, but because they're engaged in the greatest power struggle of their lives, with a view to retaining control of the future wealth of the most populous nation on earth. It suits their purposes to portray Falun Gong's practitioners as a gaggle of agitators, and Li as a malevolent foreigner. Their hope is that, if these portrayals take hold, the repression will be to a large degree justified. But that hope will not be realized, and they will have to face, as never before, the consequences of their actions.

In 1998, China took an irreversible step by signing the International Convention on Civil and Political Rights — a formal admission that human rights could indeed be linked to trade issues. That signature cannot be conveniently erased. Likewise, when China enters the WTO, it can of course demand any number of rights and privileges, but the international community can demand, in turn, that China meet (or pay lip service to) any number of obligations — a bitter pill to swallow for a country whose constitution proclaims it to be a "democratic dictatorship."

But Falun Gong's practitioners have also been defined politically by Western nations and economic interests, who have raised the human rights issue largely to suit themselves. It does no good for Li and his followers to keep on repeating that they have no political object, and that asserting their human rights is a far cry from acting as a political entity. That's true to a point, but that point was passed when Falun Gong attempted to enlist the help of the U.S. Congress and Senate, the European Parliament, and the United Nations Committee on Human Rights. Not only did Falun Gong seek official worldwide condemnation of the Chinese government's actions, it in effect demanded that Jiang's regime grant it the freedom to practise, preach, assemble, and congregate without any degree of state control whatsoever. It also made it abundantly clear that both internal and international pressures would continue to be applied until China capitulated to its demands. These, by anyone's definition, are political actions.

But these actions, too, are naive, because Falun Gong's demands will not be met. They would not be met even in the West, where every government maintains the right to deal with what it deems to be a "disruptive assembly." Western nations frequently arrest and detain peaceful protesters who do not obtain the requisite permits, or who fail to obey a police order to disperse — witness the demonstrations at the WTO meetings in Seattle, the pepper-spray-clouded APEC summit in Vancouver, and, for that matter, any old special-interest rally in any major North American city.

None of this is to excuse China's responses to Falun Gong, or to deny that they've been grotesquely extreme. But neither can it be denied that Falun Gong has consistently aimed to force the Chinese government to accept unconditionally its belief system by mustering all the international allies it can find, thus making it a political target in China and a political actor in the eyes of the West.

And with what results? For the moment, all that's certain is that China has sown the seeds of the very rebellion it's striving to quell. Falun Gong practitioners have been strengthened in their convictions, and the Chinese people at large have been offered a daily reminder of the true nature of the Communist regime. This, in turn, amplifies their contempt, disgust, and eventual resolve to get rid of the current leadership.

China's excessive actions also signal to the world that it is a brutally regressive throwback that is not yet ready to join the civilized international community, host the Olympics, participate fully in the WTO, sign international covenants, or take its place among the leading powers of the twenty-first century. In short, by continuing to oppress Falun Gong, China only guarantees the long-term repercussions it most desperately wishes to avoid, both at home and abroad.

We may or may not have come appreciably closer to understanding Li Hongzhi and Falun Gong. Theories take us only so far down that road; practices are the key. Falun Gong already has plenty of martyrs and thousands abused or wrongfully imprisoned. Li may not be particularly creative in his approach, but he senses, either instinctively or historically, that martyrdom is inextricably linked to the cause.

He is no stranger to psychology, and has embraced and perfected the most psychologically refined means of challenging the status quo — a reliance on non-violent acts that provoke violence in others. As Gandhi and Martin Luther King found, this method is spectacularly powerful in its effect on the observing world. Jiang is in for a rough ride — but so are the practitioners who march ritualistically into danger on Master Li's behalf.

Among some Falun Gong individuals, martyrdom has become an unhealthy vehicle. On May 5, 2000, the group's Minghui Web

site offered a testimonial allegedly written by a woman who identified herself as Lili Feng, a Chinese-American assistant
professor at the Scripps Research Institute in La Jolla, California
— in other words, not a peasant woman from the Chinese hinterland, but a highly intelligent and thoroughly Westernized
academic. She described her thirteen days of imprisonment in
the city of Shenzhen, where she'd gone on a family visit. Jailed
for professing her faith in Falun Gong, Ms. Feng nonetheless
preached Li's teachings to her fellow prisoners, found immediate
converts among the prostitutes and thieves, and in general succeeded in spreading goodness and light within the jail. The
wholehearted and unquestioning acceptance of the word by
those in dire circumstances left her even more impressed with the
power of her beliefs, one of which was that "Falun Gong is
worth dying for."

Whether or not the story is true, the Falun Gong disciples
who run the organization's Web sites chose to run it for a period
of time as an example of what kinds of personal sacrifice are
necessary to reach consummation. And indeed the whole
concept of consummation gathered force on October 1, 2000,
China's National Day and the fifty-first anniversary of the
founding of the People's Republic of China. A few days earlier,
Master Li had, for the first time, used his Web sites to encourage
his followers to confront the government: "I'm happy for those
who have stepped forward," he wrote on September 24 on
clearwisdom.net. "Whether they are imprisoned or lose their lives
for persevering in Dafa cultivation, they achieve consummation."

And indeed hundreds of practitioners showed up on October
1 in Tiananmen Square, where they were predictably and brutally
arrested by Jiang's police. Some have suggested that this action
by Li is no different from Martin Luther King exhorting the
civil rights marchers in the United States to continue with their
protests for freedom and equality in the southern states during

the early sixties. Perhaps, but there is an essential difference: King was at the front, leading the marchers, and was among the first to be beaten and arrested by the police.

To be fair, Li has consistently refused to be stereotyped as a political martyr. And he has always insisted that Falun Gong is a belief system in which practitioners must "forebear" — with or without him as leader.

Bibliography

Basser, Stephen. "Acupuncture, the Facts," *National Journal of Australian Skeptics* 13 (March 1993).

Batchelor, Stephen. *The Awakening of the West: The Encounter of Buddhism and Western Culture: 543 BCE—1992*. London: Aquarian, 1994.

Becker, Jasper. "Long Road from Factory Worker to President," *South China Monitoring Post*, May 25, 1996.

Berling, Judith A. *The Syncretic Religion of Lin Chao-en*. New York: Columbia University Press, 1980.

Campbell, Joseph. *The Hero with a Thousand Faces*. Princeton: Princeton University Press, 1971.

Ch'ên, Kenneth Kuan Shêng. *Buddhism in China: A Historical Survey*. Princeton: Princeton University Press, 1964.

Ching, Julia. *Chinese Religions*. Basingstoke: Macmillan Press, 1993.

Clarke, J.J. *Jung and Eastern Thought: A Dialogue with the Orient*. London and New York: Routledge, 1994.

Conze, Edward. *Buddhism: Its Essence and Development*. New York: Harper & Row, 1959.

Dalai Lama. *Four Noble Truths: Fundamentals of the Buddhist Teachings.* Translated by Geshe Thupten Jinpa. Edited by Dominique Side. London: Thorsons, 1997.

"Jiang Zemin Personality Cult," *South China Monitoring Post,* February 15, 1995.

Joshi, Shubhada A. Lokayata. *A Critical Study: Indian Spiritualism Reaffirmed,* Sri Garib Das Oriental Series, vol. I, no. 180. Delhi, India: Sri Satguru Publications, 1995.

Jung, C.G. *Jung on the East.* Edited by J.J. Clarke. London: Routledge, 1995.

Kalupahana, David J. *Buddhist Philosophy: A Historical Analysis.* Honolulu: University Press of Hawaii, 1976.

Kalupahana, David J. and Indrani Kalupahana. *The Way of Siddhartha: A Life of the Buddha.* Boulder: Shambhala Publications, 1982.

Karetzky, Patricia Eichenbaum. *The Life of the Buddha: Ancient Scriptural and Pictorial Traditions.* Lanham, Md.: University Press of America, 1992.

Lieberthal, Kenneth. *Governing China: From Revolution Through Reform.* New York: Norton, 1995.

Lifton, Robert Jay. *Destroying the World to Save It: Aum Shinrikyo, Apocalyptic Violence, and the New Global Terrorism.* New York: Metropolitan Books, 1999.

Lopez, Donald S. Jr., ed. *Religions of China in Practice.* Princeton: Princeton University Press, 1996.

Magee, Bryan. *The Philosophy of Schopenhauer.* Oxford: Clarendon Press, 1983.

Mohanty, Deba R. "Power Struggle in China: The Post-Deng Scenario and Jiang Zemin as the 'First Among Equals.'" [www.idsa-india.org./an-may8-8.html], 1998.

Nuland, Sherwin B. *The Mysteries Within: A Surgeon Reflects on Medical Myths.* New York: Simon & Schuster, 2000.

Occhiogrosso, Peter. *The Joy of Sects: A Spirited Guide to the World's Religious Traditions.* New York: Doubleday, 1994.

Rahula, Walpola. *What the Buddha Taught.* New York: Grove Press, 1974.

Robinet, Isabelle. *Taoism: Growth of a Religion*. Stanford: Stanford
   University Press, 1997.

Snelling, John. *The Elements of Buddhism*. Shaftesbury and Rockport:
   Element, 1990.

Shambaugh, David. "Deng Xiaoping: The Politician," *China Quarterly*
   135 (September 1993).

Thomas, Edward Joseph. *The Life of Buddha as Legend and History*.
   London: Routledge & Kegan Paul, 1969.

Trungpa, Chogyam. *The Myth of Freedom and the Way of Meditation*.
   Edited by John Baker and Marvin Casper. Berkeley: Shambhala,
   1976.

Wayman, Alex. *Buddhist Insight: Essays by Alex Wayman*. Edited by
   George Elder. Delhi: Motilal Banarsidass, 1984.

Zeyl, Donald J., Daniel T. Devereux and Phillip T. Mitsis, eds.
   Encyclopedia of Classical Philosophy. London: Fitzroy Dearborn,
   1996.

Index